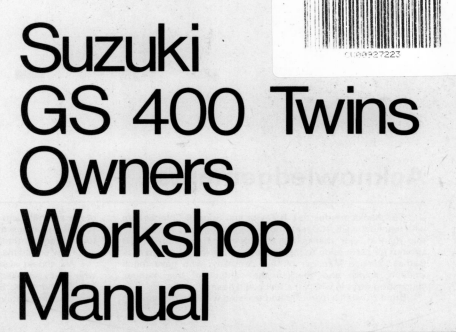

Suzuki
GS 400 Twins
Owners
Workshop
Manual

by Mansur Darlington

Models covered:

GS 400 and
GS 400B   398 cc first imported UK 1977, USA 1977
GS 400C   398 cc first imported UK 1978, USA 1978
GS 400XB   398 cc first imported USA 1977
GS 400XC   398 cc first imported USA 1978

ISBN 0 85696 415 8

HAYNES PUBLISHING GROUP
SPARKFORD YEOVIL SOMERSET ENGLAND
distributed in the USA by
HAYNES PUBLICATIONS INC
861 LAWRENCE DRIVE
NEWBURY PARK
CALIFORNIA 91320
USA

Acknowledgements

Our thanks are due to P R Taylor and Sons of Chippenham who loaned the GS 400 featured in the photographs throughout this manual. Our thanks are also due to Heron Suzuki GB Limited for permission to reproduce their drawings, and to Nick Barnes, Service Manager of that company, who gave much valuable advice and checked the content of this manual, suggesting ways in which the text could be improved.

Brian Horsfall supervised and assisted with the dismantling of the machine and also the rebuilding sequences, and devised various ingenious methods for overcoming the lack of service tools. Leon Martindale arranged and took the photographs and Jeff Clew edited the text.

We should also like to thank the Avon Rubber Company who kindly supplied us with information and advice about tyre fitting, and NGK Spark Plugs (UK) Ltd for information and photographs relating to spark plug conditions.

About this manual

The author of this manual is convinced that the only way meaningful and easy to follow text can be written, is to do the work himself, under conditions that exist in the ordinary household. As a result, the hands seen in the photographs are those of the author. Suzuki service tools have not been used. We have proved that there are ways of removing or slackening vital components when special tools are not available, providing this is done carefully and a reasonable amount of time is allowed. Risk of damage must be avoided at all costs.

Each of the 6 Chapters is divided into numbered Sections. Within the Sections are numbered paragraphs. In consequence cross reference throughout the manual is both straightfoward and logical. When a reference is made "See Section 2.8" it means Section 2, paragraph 8 in the same Chapter. If another

Chapter were meant the text would read "See Chapter 6, Section 2.8".

All photographs are captioned with a Section/paragraph number to which they refer and are always relevant to the Chapter text adjacent. Figure numbers (usually line drawings) appear in numerical order, within a given Chapter. Fig. 1.1 therefore refers to the first figure in Chapter 1. Left-hand and right-hand descriptions of the parts of the machine apply when the rider is seated on the machine in the normal riding position.

Whilst every care is taken to ensure that the information in this manual is correct, no liability can be accepted by the author or publishers for loss, damage or injury, caused by any errors in or omissions from the information given.

Introduction to the Suzuki GS 400 models

Although the Suzuki Motor Company Limited commenced manufacturing motorcycles as early as 1936, it was not until 1963 that their machines were first imported into the UK. The first of the twin cylinder models, the T10, became available during 1964 and it was immediately obvious that this particular model would be well-received by holders of a provisional driving licence, who are restricted to an engine capacity limit of 250 cc. Not many 250 cc motorcycles at that period were capable of a genuine near 90 mph maximum speed and yet able to show a fuel consumption figure well in excess of 100 mpg. An electric starter and an hydraulic rear brake were additional attractions.

The number of models available from Suzuki increased steadily until 1971 when one could choose a model from machines ranging in capacity from 50 cc to 750 cc. All these machines had one characteristic in common; the two-stroke engine upon which Suzuki built their reputation.

In line with the modern trend, Suzuki have introduced a range of four-strokes to compete with their major competitors. The GS400, which fills the mid-market requirement for an economical but sporting mount which can be used both as a commuting and a touring machine, was introduced at the same time as the GS750 and the GS550 models. Although the latter are four-cylinder machines, the two cylinder GS400 has many components in common with these and is designed around the same fundamental concept.

The 400 Suzuki is available in two forms. The first, known as the GS400 (later versions being the GS400B and C) was the first of the type, being fited with a disc front brake and electric starting. Soon after introduction the original model was supplemented by the GS400XB. This machine, styled and produced as an economy model, is similar in most respects, but is fitted with a twin leading shoe front brake in place of the disc, and has no provision for electric starting. In addition, some parts of the electrical system differ, particularly the instrument panel display.

Instructions in this manual relating to electric start components should be disregarded where the machine being attended to is the GS400XB.

Contents

Note: General description and specifications are given in each Chapter immediately after list of contents.
Fault diagnosis is given at the end of the Chapter.

1978 Suzuki GS400 model

1978 Suzuki GS400 model

Ordering spare parts

When ordering spare parts for any Suzuki, it is advisable to deal direct with an official Suzuki agent who should be able to supply most of the parts ex-stock. Parts cannot be obtained from Suzuki direct and all orders must be routed via an approved agent even if the parts required are not held in stock. Always, quote the engine and frame numbers in full, especially if parts are required for earlier models.

The frame and engine numbers are stamped on a Manufacturer's Plate riveted to the steering head on the left hand side. The frame number is also stamped on the frame itself on the right-hand side of the steering head. The engine number is stamped on the upper crankcase.

Use only genuine Suzuki spares. Some pattern parts are available that are made in Japan and may be packed in similar looking packages. They should only be used if genuine parts are hard to obtain or in an emergency, for they do not normally last as long as genuine parts, even although there may be a price advantage.

Some of the more expendable parts such as spark plugs, bulbs, tyres, oils and greases etc., can be obtained from accessory shops and motor factors, who have convenient opening hours and can often be found not far from home. It is also possible to obtain parts on a Mail Order basis from a number of specialists who advertise regularly in the motor cycle magazines.

Location of Frame number

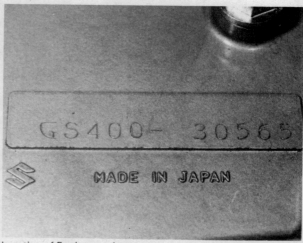

Location of Engine number

Routine maintenance

Periodic routine maintenance is a continuous process that commences immediately the machine is used and continues until the machine is no longer fit for service. It must be carried out at specified mileage recordings or on a calendar basis if the machine is not used regularly, whichever is the sooner. Maintenance should be regarded as an insurance policy, to help keep the machine in the peak of condition and to ensure long, trouble-free service. It has the additional benefit of giving early warning of any faults that may develop and will act as a safety check, to the obvious advantage of both rider and machine alike.

The various maintenance tasks are described under their respective mileage and calendar headings. Accompanying photos or diagrams are provided, where necessary. It should be remembered that the interval between the various maintenance tasks serves only as a guide. As the machine gets older, is driven hard, or is used under particularly adverse conditions, it is advisable to reduce the period between each check.

For ease of reference each service operation is described in detail under the relevant heading. However, if further general information is required it can be found within the manual in the relevant Chapter.

Although no special tools are required for routine maintenance, a good selection of general workshop tools is essential. Included in the tools must be a range of metric ring or combination spanners, a selection of crosshead screwdrivers, and two pairs of circlip pliers, one external opening and the other internal opening. Additionally, owing to the extreme tightness of most casing screws on Japanese machines, an impact screwdriver, together with a choice of large or small cross-head screw bits, is absolutely indispensable. This is particularly so if the engine has not been dismantled since leaving the factory.

Weekly or every 200 miles

Tyre pressures

1   Check the tyre pressures with a pressure gauge that is known to be accurate. Always check the pressures when the tyres are cold. If the tyres are checked after the machine has travelled a number of miles, the tyres will have become hot and consequently the pressure will have increased, possibly as much as 8 psi. A false reading will therefore always result.

		Solo	Pillion
Tyre pressures:	Front tyre	25 psi (1.75 kg/cm²)	25 psi (1.75 kg/cm²)
	Rear tyre	28 psi (2.0 kg/cm²)	32 psi (2.25 kg/cm²)

Engine oil level

2   Place the machine on the centre stand and by viewing the sight-glass in the primary drive casing, check that the engine/transmission oil level is between the two level marks. The machine must be upright because even a slight lean will give a false reading. If necessary, replenish the engine with the correct quantity of SAE 20W/50 engine oil. The filler cap is situated in the top of the primary drive cover. Allow at least 2 minutes after stopping engine before checking level.

Check oil level with machine absolutely vertical

Replenish with engine oil of correct specification

Safety check

3   Give the machine a close visual inspection, checking for loose nuts and fittings, frayed control cables etc.

Legal check

4   Ensure that the lights, horn and traffic indicators function correctly, also the speedometer.

Final drive chain lubrication

5   In order that final drive chain life be extended as much as possible regular lubrication and adjustment is essential. This is particularly so when the chain is not enclosed or is fitted to a machine transmitting high power to the rear wheel.

Intermediate lubrication should take place at the weekly or 200 mile service with the chain in position on the machine. The chain may be lubricated whilst it is on the machine by the application of one of the proprietary chain greases contained in an aerosol can. Ordinary engine oil can be used, though owing to the speed with which it is flung off the rotating chain, its effective life is limited.

Monthly or every 500 miles

Complete the tasks listed under the weekly/200 mile heading and then carry out the following checks:

Tyre damage

1   Rotate each wheel and check for damage to the tyres, especially splitting on the sidewalls. Remove any stones or other objects caught between the treads. This is particularly important on the front tyre, where rapid tyre deflation due to penetration of the inner tube will almost certainly cause total loss of control of the machine.

Spoke tension

2   Check the spokes for tension, by gently tapping each one with a metal object. A loose spoke is identifiable by the low pitch noise emitted when struck. If any one spoke needs considerable tightening, it will be necessary to remove the tyre and inner tube in order to file down the protruding spoke end. This will prevent it from chafing through the rim band and piercing the inner tube.

Hydraulic fluid level – disc brake models

3   Check the level of the hydraulic fluid in the master cylinder reservoir mounted on the handlebars. The level can be seen through the transparent reservoir and should be between the upper and lower level marks. Ensure that the handlebars are in the central position when a level reading is taken and also when the cap and diaphragm are removed. Replenish the reservoir with an hydraulic fluid of the following specifications:

DOT 3 or DOT 4 (USA)
SAE J1703a, b or c
SAE 70R3 may also be used   (UK)

Care should be taken that a specified fluid is used. An incorrect fluid may perish the piston seals and cause brake failure.

Rear brake adjustment

4   When the rear brake is in correct adjustment the total brake pedal travel measured at the toe tread should be within the range 20 – 30 mm (0.8 – 1.2 in). If the travel is greater or less than this, carry out the necessary adjustment by means of the shouldered nut at the brake arm end of the cable.

Front brake adjustment – drum brake models

5   Adjust the operating cable at the handlebar lever so that there is approximately 1 in (25 mm) movement at the lever end before brake action is commenced.

If braking efficiency has deteriorated due to uneven shoe wear or wear of the operating link or arms, adjustment should be carried out by referring to the procedure in Chapter 5, Section 10.

Final drive chain adjustment

6   Check the slack in the final drive chain. The correct up and down movement, as measured at the mid-point of the chain lower run, should be 15 – 20 mm (0.6 – 0.8 in). Adjustment should be carried out as follows: Place the machine on the centre stand so that the rear wheel is clear of the ground and free to rotate. Remove the split pin from the wheel spindle and slacken the wheel nut a few turns. Loosen the locknuts on the two chain adjuster bolts, and slacken off the brake torque rod nuts.

Rotation of the adjuster bolts in a clockwise direction will tighten the chain. Tighten each bolt a similar number of turns so that wheel alignment is maintained. This can be verified by checking that the mark on the outer face of each chain adjuster is aligned with the same aligning mark on each fork end. With the adjustment correct, tighten the wheel nut and fit a new split pin. Finally, retighten the adjuster bolt locknuts, and tighten the torque rod nuts, securing them by means of the split pins.

Apply chain lubricant with chain in place

Verify brake fluid level and replenish, if required.

Battery electrolyte level

7   Access to the battery may be made after removal of the frame left-hand side cover.

 The electrolyte solution should be between the upper and lower level lines. If the electrolyte solution is low it should be replenished, using distilled water.

Three monthly or every 1500 miles

 Complete the checks listed under the preceding Routine Maintenance Sections and then complete the following:

Engine/transmission oil change

1   Drain the engine oil by removing the drain plug from the underside of the sump and the filler cap from the top of the primary drive cover. Unscrew also the oil filter chamber drain plug to allow the small amount of lubricant within to escape. It is preferable to complete this task when the engine has reached normal running temperature. The oil will be thinner and so flow more easily. Ensure that a container of sufficient size is placed below the engine to catch the oil. When all the oil has drained off, refit and tighten the drain plugs, after checking that their sealing washers are in good condition. Replenish the engine with approximately the following quantity of SAE 20W/50 motor oil.

 2·1 lit (4·4/3·6 US/Imp pint)

 Allow the oil to settle and then check the level by means of the sight-glass. Add more lubricant, if necessary.

Final drive chain lubrication

2   Lubrication of the rear chain should be carried out at short intervals as described in Section 5 of the Weekly or 200 mile maintenance schedule. On machines fitted with a non-standard chain using a spring joining link more thorough lubrication should be carried out with the chain off the machine. The original chain has no spring link and therefore swinging arm removal must take place before the chain can be removed. In this case it is suggested that the chain be cleaned thoroughly whilst still in position, using a proprietary degreaser such as 'Gunk' or 'Jizer' and then lubricated using graphited grease from an aerosol can. Where a chain having a spring link is used, separate the chain by removing the spring link and run it off the sprockets. If an old chain is available, interconnect the old and new chain, before the new chain is run off the sprockets. In this way the old chain can be pulled into place on the sprockets and then used to pull the regreased chain into place with ease.

 Clean the chain thoroughly in a paraffin bath and then finally with petrol. The petrol will wash the paraffin out of the links and rollers which will then dry more quickly.

 Allow the chain to dry and then immerse it in a molten lubricant such as Linklyfe or Chainguard. These lubricants must be used hot and will achieve better penetration of the links and rollers. They are less likely to be thrown off by centrifugal force when the chain is in motion.

 Refit the newly greased chain onto the sprocket, replacing the spring link. This is accomplished most easily when the free ends of the chain are pushed into mesh on the rear wheel sprocket. The spring link must be fitted so that the closed end faces the normal direction of chain travel.

General lubrication

3   Apply a grease gun to the grease nipple on the swinging arm, until grease can be seen to exude from around the thrust bearing covers on either end of the crossmember. Wipe off the excess grease.

 Apply grease or oil to the handlebar lever pivots and to the centrestand and propstand pivots.

Control cable lubrication

4   Lubricate the control cables thoroughly with motor oil or an all-purpose oil. A good method of lubricating the cables is shown in the accompanying illustration, using a plasticine funnel. This method has the disadvantage that the cables usually need removing from the machine. An hydraulic cable oiler which pressurises the lubricant overcomes this problem. Do not lubricate nylon lined cables (which may have been fitted as replacements), as the oil may cause the nylon to swell, thereby causing total cable seizure.

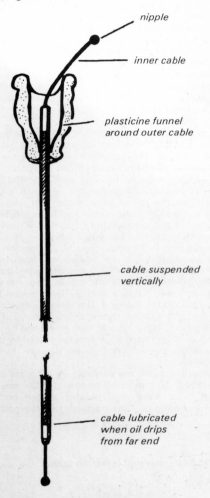

Control cable lubrication

Six monthly or 3000 miles

 Carry out the tasks described in the weekly, monthly and three monthly sections and then carry out the following:

Oil filter renewal

1   The oil filter element should be renewed at every second oil change. After draining the engine oil remove the three domed nuts from the oil filter chamber cover. The cover is under tension from the filter locating spring and so may fly off if care is not taken. Lift out the spring and oil filter element. No attempt should be made to clean the old filter; it must be discarded and a new component fitted. Clean the filter chamber before inserting the new element, which should be fitted with the rubber seal end facing inwards. Check the condition of the chamber cover sealing ring before replacing the cover.

Valve clearance checking and adjustment

2   To gain access to the camshafts and cam followers the petrol tank must be removed as described in Chapter 2, Section 2 and the camshaft cover detached. After removal of the cover bolts, the seal between the cover and the gasket may be broken by the judicious use of a rawhide mallet. Strike only those parts of the cover which are well supported by lugs.

Unscrew the spark plugs and remove the contact breaker cover from the right hand side of the engine. The clearance between each cam and cam follower must be checked and if necessary adjusted by removal of the existing adjuster pad and replacement of a pad of suitable thickness. Make the clearance check and adjustment of each valve in sequence and then continue with the next valve. Commence by rotating the engine so that the exhaust camshaft right-hand lobe is pointing vertically up. The two exhaust valve clearances can now be checked. Having done this rotate the engine a further 180° until the inlet camshaft left-hand lobe is pointing vertically up. The two inlet valve clearances can now be checked. Rotate the engine in a forward direction by means of the engine turning hexagon on the contact breaker cam end.

Using a feeler gauge determine and record the clearance at the first valve. If the clearance is incorrect, not being within the range of 0·03 – 0·08 mm (0·001 – 0·003 in), the adjuster pad must be removed and replaced by one of suitable thickness. A special tool is available ((Suzuki part No. 09916 – 64510) which may be pushed between the camshaft adjacent to the cam lobe and the raised edge of the cam follower, to allow removal of the shim. If the special tool is not available, a simple substitute may be fabricated from a portion of steel plate.

The final form of the tool which has a handle about 6 inches long, can be seen in the accompanying photograph.

The Suzuki tool may be pushed into position, depressing the cam follower and securing it in a depressed position, in one operation. Where a home-made tool is used, the cam follower may be depressed using a suitable lever placed between the adjuster pad and the camlobe. The tool may then be inserted to secure the cam follower whilst the adjuster pad is removed. Before installing either type of tool, rotate the cam follower so that the slot in the raised edge is not obscured by the camshaft. Insert a small screwdriver through the slot to displace the adjuster shim.

Adjustment pads are available in 20 sizes ranging from 2·15 mm to 3·10 mm in increments of 0·05 mm. Each pad is identified by a three digit number etched on the reverse face.The number (eg. 235) indicates that the pad thickness is 2·35 mm thick. To select the correct pad subtract 0·03 mm from the measured clearance and add the resultant figure to that of the existing pad. Select the largest available pad whose thickness is slightly smaller than the final figure. Refer to the accompanying table for the selection of available pads.

Although the adjuster pads are available as a complete set their price is prohibitive. It is suggested that pads are purchased individually, after an accurate assessment of requirement has been made. It is possible that some Suzuki service agents will be prepared to exchange needed pads for others of the correct size, providing that the original pads are not worn.

Before installing a replacement pad, lubricate both sides thoroughly with engine oil. Always fit the pad with the identification number downwards, so that it does not become obliterated by the action of the cam. After fitting new adjuster pads, rotate the engine forwards a number of times and then recheck the clearances to verify that no errors have occurred.

Before refitting the camcover, together with a new gasket, lubricate the camshafts with copious quantities of clean engine oil.

Contact breaker adjustment

3   To gain access to the contact breaker assembly it is necessary to remove the engine right-hand cover which is retained by three screws.

Before adjusting the points, examine each set for burning or pitting. Clean or renew the points as necessary. See Section 5 of Chapter 2. The points are marked L and R adjacent to the relevant contact set, indicating the cylinder they serve.

Set the gap of points marked L first. Turn the crankshaft using a spanner on the large hexagonal washer securing the cam, until these points are fully open. Measure the gap with a feeler gauge, and adjust if necessary. Standard gap: 0·3 – 0·4 mm (0·012 – 0·16 in).

If the gap requires adjustment, slacken slightly the slotted screw which secures the fixed contact. A screwdriver should be engaged between the slot in the fixed contact, and the two pins on the contact breaker back plate; by turning the screwdriver the gap may be opened or closed. Tighten the screw and recheck the gap.

Turn the crankshaft so that the points marked R are fully open, and repeat the procedure above. Do not slacken the two screws which secure the R contact set base plate to the main base plate; this will upset the timing. It is important that both points should be set to the same gap, as the gap determines the moment when the contacts open, and thus the ignition timing.

Fig. RM2 Adjuster pad selection table

No.	Thickness (mm)	Part No.	No.	Thickness (mm)	Part No.
1	2.15	12892–45000	11	2.65	12892–45010
2	2.20	12892–45001	12	2.70	12892–45011
3	2.25	12892–45002	13	2.75	12892–45012
4	2.30	12892–45003	14	2.80	12892–45013
5	2.35	12892–45004	15	2.85	12892–45014
6	2.40	12892–45005	16	2.90	12892–45015
7	2.45	12892–45006	17	2.95	12892–45016
8	2.50	12892–45007	18	3.00	12892–45017
9	2.55	12892–45008	19	3.05	12892–45018
10	2.60	12892–45009	20	3.10	12892–45019

Remove cover to gain access to oil filter

Check cam lobe/follower clearances using a feeler gauge

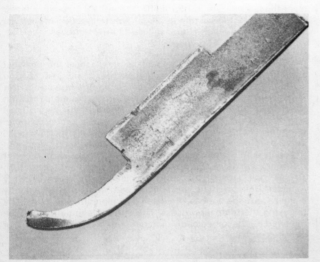
Use fabricated tool to ...

... depress cam follower and allow ...

adjuster pad removal

Each pad is marked for size

Ignition timing

4   Whenever the contact breaker unit receives attention, the ignition timing should be checked as a matter of course and adjusted, if necessary.

Apply a spanner to the engine rotation hexagon and turn the engine in a forward direction, whilst viewing the ATU through the inspection aperture in the contact breaker stator plate. It will be seen that there is a set of three scribed lines on each side of the ATU. Each side is marked 'R' or 'L' to differentiate which marks control which cylinder.

Commence ignition timing checking on the left-hand contact breaker set, which controls the left-hand cylinder. To determine at which moment the points open connect a 12v bulb between the moving point and a suitable earthing point on the engine. With the ignition turned on, the bulb will light up when the points are open. Rotate the engine until the F mark on the left-hand side of the ATU is in **exact** alignment with the index pointer mark on the casing to the rear of the stator plate. If the ignition is correct, the points should be on the verge of opening when this position is reached. This will be indicated by the flickering of the bulb.

To adjust the ignition timing on the left-hand cylinder slacken the three screws which pass through the elongated holes in the stator plate periphery. Rotate the plate until the light flickers and then tighten the screws. Turn the engine backwards about 90° and then forwards again to check the setting.

Check the ignition timing on the right-hand cylinder in a similar manner, using the F timing mark on the right-hand side of the ATU. If the timing is incorrect, slacken the two screws holding the right-hand contact breaker assembly mounting plate to the main stator plate. Move the plate to the correct position and tighten the screws. Recheck the timing.

Provided that the contact breakers are in good condition and care is taken, manual adjustment of the ignition timing should be acceptably accurate. If possible, however, the timing should be checked using a stroboscope lamp.

Check and adjust the 1·4 contact breaker first and then the 2·3 contact breaker. At 1500 rpm and below, the F mark should align with the index mark. Full advance should be reached at 3600 rpm, when the unmarked advance line to the right of the F mark should be in line with the index mark. Adjustment should be made in the same manner as described for manual ignition timing.

Before replacing the contact breaker cover, apply a small quantity of light oil or grease to the cam lubricating wick. Do not overlubricate, as excess oil may find its way onto the points, causing ignition failure.

Carburettor synchronisation

5   In order that the engine maintains the best possible performance at all times the carburettors must always remain correctly adjusted and synchronised. This check is essential and should be carried out at the specified intervals.

Synchronisation and adjustment of the carburettors requires the use of a set of two vacuum gauges or indicators together with the appropriate adaptors which screw into the inlet tracts and to which are attached the vacuum take-off pipes. The adjustment of the carburettors is critical if smooth running and optimum fuel economy is to be expected and if damage to the engine due to incorrect mixture is to be avoided. Because of this and the prohibitive cost of the gauges required, it is recommended that the machine be returned to a Suzuki Service Agent, who will be able to carry out the work. If the vacuum gauges are available and some previous experience has been gained in their use, refer to Chapter 2 Section 6 for the prescribed adjustment procedure.

Cleaning and checking spark plugs

6   Remove the spark plugs and clean them, using a wire brush. Clean the electrodes using fine emery paper or cloth and then reset the gaps to 0·6 – 0·7 mm (0·024 – 0·28 in) using a feeler gauge. Before replacing the plugs, smear the threads with a small amount of graphite grease to aid future removal.

Air filter cleaning

7   To gain access to the air filter element, raise the dualseat and remove the air filter box lid, which is secured by two screws. The air filter element and carrier can be lifted out, after removal of the single carrier screw. Detach the element from the carrier by disengaging the two ends of the spring-steel retaining strip. The element is of the oil impregnated polyurethane sponge type, and should be washed thoroughly in petrol to remove all the oil and dust. After cleaning, squeeze out the sponge to remove the petrol and then allow a short time for the remaining petrol to evaporate. **Do not** wring out the sponge, as this may damage the fabric and lead to the need for early renewal. Reimpregnate the sponge with engine oil and gently squeeze out the excess. Reinstall the element and carrier by reversing the removal process. The air filter element should be renewed if it becomes badly clogged or if the sponge hardens or perishes with age.

Nine monthly or 6000 miles

Perform all the maintenance tasks listed under the preceding time/mileage headings and then carry out the following:

Adjust points gap with points FULLY OPEN

Lubricate lightly the felt wick

Air filter element is secured by spring-steel strip

Wash element in petrol and reimpregnate

Spark plug renewal

1 Remove and discard the existing spark plugs regardless of their condition. Although the plugs may give acceptable performance after they have reached this mileage, it is unlikely that they are still working at peak efficiency.

The correct spark plugs are NGK B8ES or Nippon Denso W24ES. Before fitting the new plugs, adjust the gap of each to 0·6 – 0·7 mm (0·024 – 0·028 in).

Front fork oil change

2 Place the machine on the centre stand so that it rests securely in a level position. The fork legs should be drained and refilled one at a time, so that the fork leg not being attended to will support the weight of the machine.

Remove the clamps holding the handlebars to the top fork yoke so that access may be made to the fork stanchion end bolts. Place a container below the fork leg drain bolt which is situated above and to the rear of the wheel spindle clamp. Remove the top bolt and the drain plug.

Allow the damping fluid to drain and then pump the forks up and down to drain any residual oil. Replace and tighten the drain plug after checking that the sealing washer is in good condition. Replenish the fork leg with the following amount of fluid.

160 cc (5·5/4·5 US/Imp fl oz)

Suzuki recommend that the damping fluid be a 50/50 mixture of fork oil or ATF (automatic transmission fluid) and 10W/30 engine oil. After filling, refit the top bolt and the drain plug, and attend to the second fork leg in a similar way.

Oil filter gauze cleaning

3 When renewing the oil at this service interval the forward cover on the sump should be removed and the oil pick-up strainer screen detached for cleaning. The screen is secured to the pick-up chamber by two screws at the forward edge and a bent tag at the rear. After removing the two screws turn the screen in an anticlockwise direction to release the tag. Wash the screen in clean petrol, using a soft brush.

Yearly or every 10 000 miles

Again complete the checks listed under the previous routine maintenance interval headings. The following additional tasks are now necessary:

1 Dismantle and clean the carburettors (see Chapter 3, Sections 4 – 6.

2 Check the condition of the contact breaker assemblies and renew if necessary (See Chapter 3, Section 5).

3 Remove the front wheel and the rear wheel and examine the brake shoes for wear (front wheel, drum brake models only). (See Chapter 5, Sections 9 and 13).

4 Remove and clean the wheel bearings. Renew worn bearings. Replace bearings and repack with grease. (See Chapter 5, Sections 11 and 15). Refit both wheels.

General adjustments and examination

Clutch adjustment

1 The intervals at which the clutch should be adjusted will depend on the style of riding and the conditions under which the machine is used.

Adjust the clutch in two stages to ensure smooth operation as follows:

Remove the clutch adjustment cover which is retained by two cross-head screws, loosen the locknut on the cable adjuster, where it enters the cover, and screw the adjuster inwards approximately 6 turns, to give plenty of slack in the cable.

Loosen the locknut on the lifting mechanism adjuster screw and screw the adjuster inwards until a resistance can be felt. To give the necessary running clearance, unscrew the adjuster $\frac{1}{4}$ – $\frac{1}{2}$ a turn and then tighten the locknut. The cable should be adjusted so that there is 4 mm ($\frac{1}{16}$ in) play measured between the stock and handlebar lever, before the clutch commences lifting. Finally tighten the locknut on the clutch cable and replace the adjustment cover and gasket.

Checking front brake pad wear

2 Brake pad wear depends largely on the conditions in which the machine is ridden and at what speed. It is difficult therefore to give precise inspection intervals, but it follows that pad wear should be checked more frequently on a hard ridden machine.

The condition of each pad can be checked easily whilst still on the machine. The pads have a red groove around their outer periphery which can be seen from the front of the caliper unit. If wear has reduced either or both pads in the caliper down to the red line the pads should be renewed as a pair.

Removal and replacement of the brake pads may be accomplished without removing the respective wheel.

To gain access to the front brake pads for renewal, the caliper unit must be detached from the fork leg, although separation of the caliper from the hydraulic hose is not required. Remove the two bolts which pass through the fork leg into the caliper support bracket and lift the complete caliper unit upwards, off the disc. Remove the single screw and the convolute backing plate from the inner side of the caliper body.

The inner pad is now free and may be displaced towards the centre of the caliper, and lifted out. The outer pad, which abuts against the caliper piston, is not retained positively and may be lifted out. Refit the new pads after coating lightly the periphery of each pad with disc brake assembly grease (silicon grease). Use the grease sparingly ensuring that it **does not** come in contact with the friction surface of the pad. If necessary, push the piston inwards to increase the clearance between the pads and allow the pads to fit over the disc.

Summary of routine maintenance adjustments and capacities

Spark plug .... NGK B8ES or Nippon Denso W24ES
Spark plug gap .... 0.6 – 0.7 mm (0.024 – 0.028 in)
Contact breaker gap .... 0.35 mm (0.014 in)

Tyre pressures
Solo   Pillion
  Front 25 psi (1.75 kg–cm^2) .... 25 psi (1.75 kg – cm^2)
  Rear 28 psi (2.0 kg – cm^2) .... 32 psi (2.25 kg – cm^2)

Valve clearance (cold) .... 0.03 – 0.08 mm (0.001 – 0.003 in)

Recommended lubricants

Components	Viscosity/Product	Quantity
Engine/transmission	20W/50 engine oil	2.1 lit (4.4/3.6 US/Imp pints)
Front forks	50/50 mixture of fork oil (or ATF) and 10W/30 engine oil	160 cc (5.4/4.5 US/Imp fl oz)
Disc brakes	Brake fluid conforming to DOT 3 (US) or SAE J1703 (UK) Specifications	As required
Grease points	High melting point grease	As required

Dimensions

Overall length .... 2085 mm (82.1 in)

Overall width .... 835 mm (32.9 in)

Overall height .... 1110 mm (43.7 in)

Wheel base .... 1385 mm (54.5 in)

Weight .... 172 kg (379 lb)

Working conditions and tools

When a major overhaul is contemplated, it is important that a clean, well-lit working space is available, equipped with a workbench and vice, and with space for laying out or storing the dismantled assemblies in an orderly manner where they are unlikely to be disturbed. The use of a good workshop will give the satisfaction of work done in comfort and without haste, where there is little chance of the machine being dismantled and reassembled in anything other than clean surroundings. Unfortunately, these ideal working conditions are not always practicable and under these latter circumstances when improvisation is called for, extra care and time will be needed.

The other essential requirement is a comprehensive set of good quality tools. Quality is of prime importance since cheap tools will prove expensive in the long run if they slip or break and damage the components to which they are applied. A good quality tool will last a long time, and more than justify the cost. The basis of any tool kit is a set of open-ended spanners, which can be used on almost any part of the machine to which there is reasonable access. A set of ring spanners makes a useful addition, since they can be used on nuts that are very tight or where access is restricted. Where the cost has to be kept within reasonable bounds, a compromise can be effected with a set of combination spanners – open-ended at one end and having a ring of the same size on the other end. Socket spanners may also be considered a good investment, a basic $\frac{3}{8}$ in or $\frac{1}{2}$ in drive kit comprising a ratchet handle and a small number of socket heads, if money is limited. Additional sockets can be purchased, as and when they are required. Provided they are slim in profile, sockets will reach nuts or bolts that are deeply recessed. When purchasing spanners of any kind, make sure the correct size standard is purchased. Almost all machines manufactured outside the UK and the USA have metric nuts and bolts, whilst those produced in Britain have BSF or BSW sizes. The standard used in the USA is AF, which is also found on some of the later British machines. Other tools that should be included in the kit are a range of crosshead screwdrivers, a pair of pliers and a hammer.

When considering the purchase of tools, it should be remembered that by carrying out the work oneself, a large proportion of the normal repair cost, made up by labour charges, will be saved. The economy made on even a minor overhaul will go a long way towards the improvement of a tool kit.

In addition to the basic tool kit, certain additional tools can prove invaluable when they are close to hand, to help speed up a multitude of repetitive jobs. For example, an impact screwdriver will ease the removal of screws that have been tightened by a similar tool, during assembly, without a risk of damaging the screw heads. And, of course, it can be used again to retighten the screws, to ensure an oil or airtight seal results. Circlip pliers have their uses too, since gear pinions, shafts and similar components are frequently retained by circlips that are not too easily displaced by a screwdriver. There are two types of circlip pliers, one for internal and one for external circlips. They may also have straight or right-angled jaws.

One of the most useful of all tools is the torque wrench, a form of spanner that can be adjusted to slip when a measured amount of force is applied to any bolt or nut. Torque wrench settings are given in almost every modern workshop or service manual, where the extent is given to which a complex component, such as a cylinder head, can be tightened without fear of distortion or leakage. The tightening of bearing caps is yet another example. Overtightening will stretch or even break bolts, necessitating extra work to extract the broken portions.

As may be expected, the more sophisticated the machine, the greater is the number of tools likely to be required if it is to be kept in first class condition by the home mechanic. Unfortunately there are certain jobs which cannot be accomplished successfully without the correct equipment and although there is invariably a specialist who will undertake the work for a fee, the home mechanic will have to dig more deeply in his pocket for the purchase of similar equipment if he does not wish to employ the services of others. Here a word of caution is necessary, since some of these jobs are best left to the expert. Although an electrical multimeter of the AVO type will prove helpful in tracing electrical faults, in inexperienced hands it may irrevocably damage some of the electrical components if a test current is passed through them in the wrong direction. This can apply to the synchronisation of twin or multiple carburettors too, where a certain amount of expertise is needed when setting them up with vacuum gauges. These are, however, exceptions. Some instruments, such as a strobe lamp, are virtually essential when checking the timing of a machine powered by CDI ignition system. In short, do not purchase any of these special items unless you have the experience to use them correctly.

Although this manual shows how components can be removed and replaced without the use of special service tools (unless absolutely essential), it is worthwhile giving consideration to the purchase of the more commonly used tools if the machine is regarded as a long term purchase. Whilst the alternative methods suggested will remove and replace parts without risk of damage, the use of the special tools recommended and sold by the manufacturer will invariably save time.

Chapter 1 Engine, gearbox and clutch

Contents

Specifications

Engine

Type	Parallel twin cylinder, air-cooled, dohc, four-stroke
Cubic Capacity	398 cc (24.3 cu in)
Bore	65.0 mm (2.56 in)
Stroke	60.0 mm (2.36 in)
Compression ratio	9.0:1
bhp	36 @ 8,500 rpm

Pistons and rings
Piston diameter . . . . 64.945 - 64.960 mm (2.5569 - 2.5575 in)
Service limit . . . . 64.800 mm (2.5512 in)
Piston oversizes available . . . . 0.5 mm (0.020 in) and 1.0 mm (0.040 in)
Ring/groove clearance:
  Top and 2nd ring . . . . 0.020 - 0.055 mm (0.0008 - 0.0022 in)
  Service limit . . . . 0.18 mm (0.071 in)
  Oil control ring
  Service limit . . . . 0.15 mm (0.006 in)
Ring end gap
  Top and 2nd ring . . . . 0.1 - 0.3 mm (0.004 - 0.012 in)
  Service limit . . . . 0.6 mm (0.024 in)

Cylinder block
Bore diameter . . . . 65.00 - 65.015 mm (2.5591 - 2.5596 in)
Service limit . . . . 65.100 mm (2.5630 in)
Cylinder/piston clearance . . . . 0.050 - 0.060 mm (0.0020 - 0.0024 in)

Valves and springs
Valve stem diameter:
  Inlet . . . . 6.965 - 6.980 mm (0.2742 - 0.2748 in)
  Service limit . . . . 6.90 mm (0.2717 in)
  Exhaust . . . . 6.955 - 6.970 mm (0.2738 - 0.2744 in)
  Service limit . . . . 6.805 mm (0.2679 in)
Valve guide clearance:
  Inlet . . . . 0.02 - 0.05 mm (0.008 - 0.0020 in)
  Service limit . . . . 0.09 mm (0.0035in)
  Exhaust . . . . 0.03 - 0.06 mm (0.0012 - 0.0024 in)
  Service limit . . . . 0.10 mm (0.0039 in)
Spring free length (Nihon Hatsujo)
  Inner . . . . 37.00 mm (1.457 in)
  Service limit . . . . 33.8 mm (1.331 in)
  Outer . . . . 43.25 mm (1.703 in)
  Service limit . . . . 41.50 mm (1.634 in)
Spring free length (Chuoh Hatsujo)
  Inner . . . . 35.30 mm (1.390 in)
  Service limit . . . . 33.8 mm (1.331 in)
  Outer . . . . 43.00 mm (1.693 in)
  Service limit . . . . 41.50 mm (1.634 in)

Valve timing

	400 and 400B	400C
Inlet opens	30° BTDC	26° BTDC
Inlet closes	70° ABDC	66°ABDC
Exhaust opens	70° BBDC	66° BBDC
Exhaust closes	30° ATDC	26° ATDC

Camshaft

	400 and 400B	400C
Cam height: Inlet	36.265 - 36.295 mm (1.4278 - 1.4289) in	36.485 - 36.515 mm (1.4364 - 1.4376 in)
Service limit	36.150 mm (1.4232 in)	36.370 mm (1.4319 in)
Exhaust	35.735 - 35.765 mm (1.4069 - 1.4081 in)	36.085 - 36.115 mm (1.4207 - 1.4219 in)
Service limit	35.600 mm (1.4016 in)	35.950 mm (1.4154 in)

Camshaft/journal clearance . . . . . . 0.020 - 0.054 mm (0.0008 - 0.0021 in)
Service limit . . . . 0.150 mm (0.0059 in)
Cam bearing ID . . . . 21.959 - 21.980 mm (0.8645 - 0.8654 in)
Tappet clearance (Cold)
  Inlet and exhaust . . . . 0.03 - 0.08 mm (0.0012 - 0.0031 in)

Crankshaft
Main bearing radial clearance . . . . 0.015 - 0.040 mm (0.0006 - 0.0016 in)
Service limit . . . . 0.08 mm (0.0031 in)
Connecting rod axial clearance . . . . 0.10 - 0.65 mm (0.004 - 0.026 in)
ervice limit . . . . 1.0 mm (0.04 in)
Connecting rod deflection (max) . . . . 3 mm (0.12 in)
Crankshaft runout (max) . . . . 0.06 mm (0.0024 in)

Clutch
Type . . . . Wet, multi-plate
No of plates:
  plain 6
  friction 6

Friction plate thickness	2.9 - 3.1 mm (0.114 - 0.122 in)
Service limit	2.7 mm (0.106 in)
Plain plate distortion (max)	0.3 mm (0.12 in)
No of springs	6
Spring free length	38.4 mm (1.51 in)
Service limit	37.0 mm (1.46 in)

Gearbox

Type	Six-speed, constant mesh
Ratios	
1st gear	2.461:1
2nd gear	1.777:1
3rd gear	1.380:1
4th gear	1.125:1
5th gear	0.961:1
6th gear	0.851:1
Primary reduction	2.714:1 (76/28T)
Final reduction	2.812:1 (45/16T)

Main torque wrench settings

Cylinder head cover bolt	0.7 - 1.1 kg m (5.1 - 7.9 lb ft)
Cylinder head nut	3.5 - 3.9 kg m (25.4 - 28.2 lb ft)
Cylinder head bolt	0.7 - 1.1 kg m (5.1 - 7.9 lb ft)
Camshaft sprocket bolt	1.0 kg m (7.2 lb ft)
Camshaft bearing cap bolt	0.8 - 1.2 kg m (5.8 - 8.6 lb ft)
Crankcase bolt (6 mm)	1.0 kg m (7.2 lb ft)
Crankcase bolt (8 mm)	2.0 kg m (14.5 lb ft)
Alternator rotor bolt	6.0 - 7.0 kg m (43.4 - 50.6 lb ft)
ATU centre bolt	1.3 - 2.3 kg m (9.5 - 16.5 lbft)
Oil filter chamber nut	0.6 - 0.8 kg m (4.4 - 5.6 lb ft)

1 General description

The engine fitted to the Suzuki GS 400 series is a double overhead camshaft vertical parallel twin. The crankshaft is of the pressed-up type using four full flywheels with two crankpins arranged at 180° to one another. It runs on four main bearings of which the right-hand most is a journal ball bearing and the remaining three are caged roller bearings.

To reduce engine vibration, a single balance shaft is fitted within the crankcase, mounted forward of the crankshaft and supported on a journal ball bearing at either end. The balance shaft is driven by a pinion mounted on the crankshaft, inboard of the primary drive pinion.

The camshaft drive chain, which is driven from a sprocket mounted centrally on the crankshaft, passes upwards through a tunnel in the cylinder block to the inlet and exhaust camshafts mounted on the cylinder head. The chain is maintained in correct tension by an automatic tensioner unit bolted to the rear of the cylinder block.

The valves are operated by the cam lobes via in-line bucket type cam followers, fitted with removable hardened pads for valve clearance adjustment.

The crankcases, which house the crankshaft and gearbox components, separate in the horizontal plane to facilitate easy dismantling and reassembly. Wet sump lubrication is supplied by a gear driven trochoidal pump, the oil passing through a wire gauze trap and paper filter element under pressure to all working surfaces of the engine.

The multi-plate clutch is fitted to the right-hand side of the engine, primary drive being through two spur gears. A six speed constant mesh gearbox then transmits power through a roller chain to the rear wheel.

2 Operation with engine/gearbox in frame

It is not necessary to remove the engine unit from the frame in order to dismantle the following items:
1 Right and left-hand crankcase covers and final drive sprocket cover.

2 Clutch assembly and gear selector components (external).
3 Oil pump and filter.
4 Alternator and starter motor (where fitted).
5 Cylinder head and cylinder head cover.
6 Cylinder block, pistons and rings.

3 Operations with engine/gearbox unit removed from frame

As previously described the crankshaft and gearbox assemblies are housed within a common casing. Any work carried out on either of these two major assemblies will necessitate removal of the engine from the frame so that the crankcases can be separated.

4 Removing the engine/gearbox unit

1 Place the machine on its centre stand making sure that it is standing firmly. Although by no means essential it is useful to raise the machine a number of feet above floor level by placing it on a long bench or horizontal ramp. This will enable most of the work to be carried out in an upright position, which is eminently more comfortable than crouching or kneeling in a puddle of sump oil.

2 Place a suitable receptacle below the crankcase and drain off the engine oil. The sump plug lies to the rear of the oil filter housing. The oil will drain at a higher rate if the engine has been warmed up previously, thereby heating and thinning the oil. Approximately 2 litres (4 pints) should drain out.

3 Hinge up the dualseat and remove the tool tray. Detach both frame side covers, each of which is secured at the lower edge by a single screw, and at the upper edge on two hooks projecting from the frame. Disconnect the battery by removing the positive lead (Red). If the machine is expected to be unused for any extended length of time the battery should be removed and given an external charge at approximately one month intervals (see Chapter 6 Section 7).

4 Turn the fuel tap to the 'On' or 'Reserve' position and

disconnect the petrol feed pipe and the vacuum pipe from the tap unions. The petrol pipe is secured by a spring clip, the ears of which should be pinched together to release the tension before freeing the pipe.

5   The petrol tank is supported at the forward end by two cups welded to the underside of the tank which engage with two rubber buffers either side of the frame main top tube. The rear of the tank is secured by a single bolt passing through a lug projecting from the rear. To remove the tank, unscrew the bolt and ease the tank backwards until it leaves the rubber buffers. Lift the tank up and away from the machine. Drainage of the tank before removal is not strictly necessary, although the resulting weight reduction will facilitate lifting. To drain the tank, connect a suitable length of tubing to the tap union and turn the lever to the 'prime' position to allow an unrestricted flow of fuel.

6   Detach the suppressor caps from the spark plugs and secure them to the upper frame-tubes. Disconnect the leads from the alternator, gear indicator and neutral switch and contact breaker at the relevant snap or block connectors after tracking the wires back from the engine. The alternator snap connectors are located to the rear of the battery box, and are protected by a rubber shroud. Disconnect also the heavy starter motor cable at the starter solenoid mounted behind the left-hand frame cover. Remove all the cable restraining clips or straps and pull the cables down towards the engine so that they will not become snagged during engine removal.

7   Remove the breather tube from the unions at the airfilter box and cylinder head breather cover. The tube is held at each end by a spring clip. Slacken off the screw clips which secure the carburettors to the inlet stubs and air hoses, and the air hoses to the air filter box. To give sufficient clearance for carburettor removal, the inlet stubs must be detached from the cylinder head and removed together with the two insulation blocks. Each stub and block is held by two bolts. Having detached the inlet stubs pull the carburettors forward out of the air-hoses. Tilt the carburettors up and back to clear the chain adjuster and then move the carburettors out towards the right-hand side of the machine. Before the carburettors can be removed completely, the breather and drain tubes should be released from their retaining clips and the throttle control cables detached from the operating pulley between the two instruments. Commence the latter operation by loosening the lower locknut on the forward cable adjuster. Slide the adjuster and cable out of the anchor bracket and then detach the inner cable from the pulley. Remove the rear cable in a similar manner.

8   Detach the gear lever from the splined shaft after loosening the pinch bolt. The kickstart lever, which is retained in a similar manner, can be removed at this stage or after engine removal. The lever serves as a useful handle when manoeuvring the engine from position.

9   Remove the left-hand front footrest which is secured to the frame by two bolts. Unscrew and withdraw the screws which retain the gearbox sprocket cover in place. Pull the cover from position. The clutch cable must be detached from the clutch lifting mechanism before the sprocket cover is completely freed for removal. Detach the cable inner from the lifting arm after bending down the locating tab. Slide the cable adjuster boot up the clutch cable, slacken off the adjuster locknut and unscrew the adjuster fully so that the cable can leave the casing.

10   The final drive chain fitted as standard has no master link. For this reason the chain must be detached from the engine by removing the gearbox sprocket. Bend down the sprocket nut lock washer and apply a spanner to the nut. When loosening the nut, apply the rear brake to prevent rotation of the gearbox shaft. Remove the nut and washer and then draw the sprocket off the shaft, still meshed with the chain. Disengage the sprocket and place it on one side.

11   Slacken the bolts at the exhaust pipe/silencer joint and, on 400C models, the balance pipe clamp bolts. Remove the two bolts securing each finned exhaust pipe flange to the cylinder head. The exhaust pipes may be removed individually by pulling them forwards out of the port and silencer. Silencer removal is not necessary when lifting out the engine.

12   Disconnect the tachometer drive cable at the cylinder head by unscrewing the knurled ring.

13   The engine is supported in the frame by a single bolt at the front which passes through two detachable engine plates and two bolts at the rear, the upper one of which passes through a detachable engine plate on the left-hand side. In addition, two short bolts are fitted, which pass into the underside of the crankcase and screw into triangular plate nuts restrained in recesses in the crankcase. Commence engine removal by unscrewing the two short bolts and allowing the plate nuts to fall free. Remove the nuts from the three long bolts and then detach the two forward and one rear engine plates. Push out the upper bolts carefully supporting the weight of the engine to prevent damage to the bolt threads. Note that the rear upper bolt also serves to secure the main earth lead from the battery. Remove the final bolt. Before the engine is removed from the frame check that all wiring leads are disconnected and will not get trapped or chafed. The engine is very heavy, and manoeuvring for removal requires care and patience. It is therefore advised that two stalwart assistants are on hand for this operation, one assistant being briefed to aid in the lifting and the other to give directions and help steady the cycle parts. The engine must be lifted forwards and upwards so that the sump will clear the frame lower tubes. To this end ensure that all wiring and connectors on the frame central upper tube are located out of the way so as not to obstruct the cylinder head cover. Lift the engine out from the left-hand side.

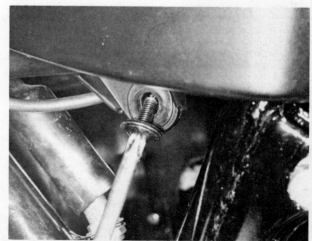
4.3 Side covers are held by single screw at lower edge

4.5 Remove single bolt and pull tank rearwards, to free

4.6 Alternator leads are connected behind battery

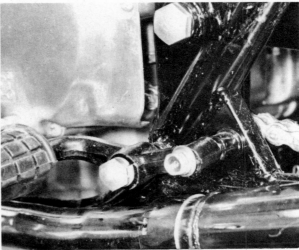
4.9a Footrest is held by two bolts

4.9b Remove sprocket cover and detach clutch cable

4.10a Bend down tab washer and remove nut

4.10b Pull off sprocket, still meshed with chain

4.11a Slacken fully the silencer/exhaust pipe clamps

4.11b Remove bolts holding flange to free pipe

4.11c Prise out and discard old ring gaskets

4.13a Unscrew short bolts holding plate nuts

4.13b Front engine plates and ...

4.13c ... rear upper left plate are detachable

4.13d Note earth cable is secured by engine bolt

4.14a Clear cables from below curve in frame tubes before ...

4.14b ... the engine is removed towards the left

5 Dismantling the engine/gearbox unit: general

1   Before commencing work on the engine unit, the external surfaces should be cleaned thoroughly. A motorcycle has very little protection from road grit and other foreign matter which sooner or later will find its way into the dismantled engine if this simple precaution is not carried out.

2   One of the proprietary cleaning compounds such as Gunk or Jizer can be used to good effect, especially if the compound is first allowed to penetrate the film of grease and oil before it is washed away. In the USA Gumout degreaser is an alternative.

3   It is essential when washing down to make sure that water does not enter the cylinder head via the ports or the electrics which are now more vulnerable.

4   If the engine has not been dismantled previously, an impact screwdriver will prove essential. This will safeguard the heads of the crosshead screws used for engine assembly. These are invariably machine-tightened during manufacture. **Caution -** Use great care as the screws and cases are easily damaged. Use a crosshead type screwdriver and NOT one of the Phillips type, which will slip out of the screws.

5   Avoid force in any of the operations. There is generally a good reason why an item is sticking, probably due to the use of the wrong procedure or sequence of operations.

6   Dismantling will be made easier if a simple engine stand is constructed that will correspond with the engine mounting points. This arrangement will permit the complete unit to be clamped rigidly to the workbench, leaving both hands free for dismantling.

6 Dismantling the engine/gearbox: removing the cylinder head cover, camshafts and tachometer drive gear

1   The breather cover, fitted to the cylinder head cover, need not be removed unless, on subsequent inspection the engine is found to have suffered extreme sludging or carbon build-up. If this is the case, the oil separator mesh inserts fitted beneath the cover should be removed and cleaned.

2   Remove the four caps which enclose the projecting ends of the camshaft and cylinder head castings. Each cap is secured by two screws. Loosen and remove the bolts securing the cylinder head cover. The bolts should be slackened evenly, in a diagonal sequence, to help prevent distortion. If necessary, use a rawhide mallet to break the seal between the cylinder head cover and the gasket, and then lift the cover away.

3   Before attention is given to the camshafts and chain, the automatic chain tensioners must be detached from the rear of

the cylinder block. The tensioner plunger within the body of the tensioner is spring loaded. Before removing the three mounting bolts, loosen the locknut on the left-hand side of the body and tighten the securing screw. This will prevent the plunger from flying out when the body is removed.

4   Remove the contact breaker cover from the right-hand engine cover to gain access to the timing marks. These are stamped on the automatic timing unit (ATU) fitted behind the contact breaker base plate. Apply a spanner to the large engine turning hexagon provided on the crankshaft end, inboard of the contact breaker cam centre bolt. Rotate the engine in a clockwise direction until the RT mark on the ATU is in line with the cast-in index mark on the casing. In this position all four cam lobes are clear of the cam followers.

5   Mark the camchain jockey wheel holder with an arrow so that on subsequent reassembly the holder and sprocket may be refitted in the same position. Remove the jockey wheel assembly after unscrewing the four retaining bolts.

6   Each camshaft should be removed separately following the same procedure. Loosen evenly the two bearing caps which locate one camshaft and lift the camshaft out to one side, complete with the sprocket. If a top-end overhaul only is anticipated, the cam chain must be prevented from falling into the crankcase when the second camshaft is removed. Place a length of dowel through the chain, lying across the cylinder head, or hook a stout piece of wire through a chain link, securing it to some convenient stud or bolt hole.

7   The tachometer drive gear housing is a push fit in the cylinder head, where it is retained by a small plate and bolt. After removal of the plate, the housing may be withdrawn together with the gearshaft.

7 Dismantling the engine/gearbox: removing the cylinder head, cylinder block, pistons and rings

1   Commence cylinder head removal by unscrewing the two small bolts adjacent to the sparking plugs. These bolts are fitted only to early models. The cylinder head bolts must be slackened evenly a little at a time by reversing the tightening sequence given in Fig. 1.17. This will prevent distortion of the large aluminium castings. Note that the four outer nuts which are domed, are fitted with copper washers. Displace the forward chain tensioner blade and withdraw it from the cam chain tunnel.

2   If necessary, use a rawhide mallet to break the seal between the cylinder head and gasket. Strike only those parts of the casting which are well supported by lugs or webs. **Under no circumstances** should levers be used to raise the head; this will

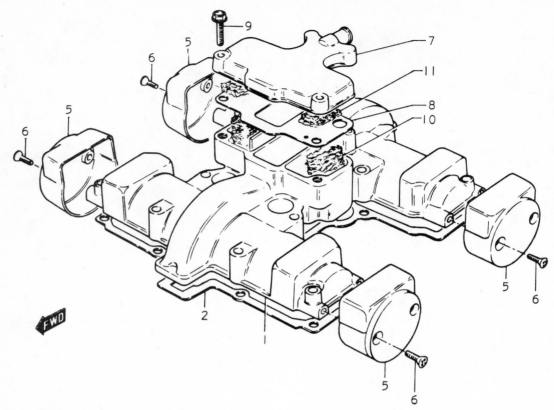

Fig. 1.1 Cylinder head cover

1 Cylinder head cover   7 Breather cover
2 Gasket   8 Gasket
3 Bolt – 8 off   9 Bolt – 4 off
4 Bolt – 4 off   10 Oil/air separator – 2 off
5 Side cover – 4 off   11 Oil/air separator – 2 off
6 Countersunk screw – 8 off

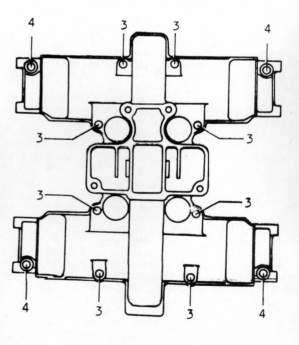

6.3 Loosen locknut and tighten screw to secure plunger

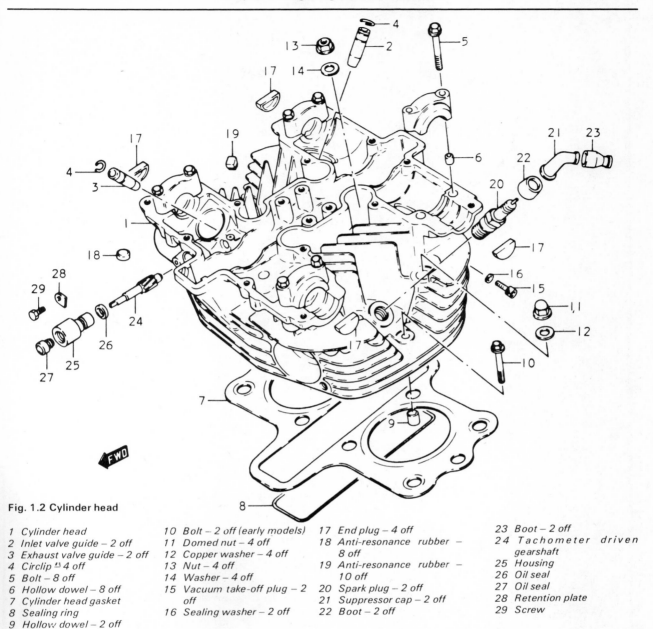

Fig. 1.2 Cylinder head

1 Cylinder head	10 Bolt – 2 off (early models)	17 End plug – 4 off	23 Boot – 2 off
2 Inlet valve guide – 2 off	11 Domed nut – 4 off	18 Anti-resonance rubber –	24 Tachometer driven
3 Exhaust valve guide – 2 off	12 Copper washer – 4 off	8 off	gearshaft
4 Circlip – 4 off	13 Nut – 4 off	19 Anti-resonance rubber –	25 Housing
5 Bolt – 8 off	14 Washer – 4 off	10 off	26 Oil seal
6 Hollow dowel – 8 off	15 Vacuum take-off plug – 2	20 Spark plug – 2 off	27 Oil seal
7 Cylinder head gasket	off	21 Suppressor cap – 2 off	28 Retention plate
8 Sealing ring	16 Sealing washer – 2 off	22 Boot – 2 off	29 Screw
9 Hollow dowel – 2 off			

result in broken fins. Where required, the cam chain should be prevented from falling down by rearranging the temporary securing wire or dowel. After lifting the cylinder head from position remove the two locating dowels, the gasket and the rectangular cam chain tunnel sealing piece.

3   Rotate the crankshaft until the two pistons are at approximately equal positions in the bore. Again using a rawhide mallet, separate the cylinder block from the base gasket. Take care not to damage the fins. Slide the cylinder block up and off the pistons taking care to support each piston as the cylinder block becomes free. If a top end overhaul only is being carried out, place a clean rag in each crankcase mouth before the lower edge of each cylinder frees the rings. This will preclude any small particles of broken ring falling into the crankcase. Invert the cylinder block and remove the two large 'O' rings, one of which fits over each protruding cylinder sleeve. Remove also the cylinder base gasket

4   Prise the outer gudgeon pin circlip of each piston from position. The gudgeon pins are a light push fit in piston bosses so

can be removed with ease. If any difficulty is encountered, apply to the offending piston crown a rag over which boiling water has just been poured. This will give the necessary temporary expansion to the piston bosses to allow the gudgeon pin to be pushed out. Before removing each piston, scribe the cylinder identification inside the piston skirt. A mark R or L will ensure that the piston is replaced in the correct bore, on reassembly. It is unnecessary to mark the back and front of the piston because this is denoted by an arrow mark cast in the piston crown.

5   Each piston is fitted with three piston rings, two compression and one oil scraper. To remove the rings, spread the ends sufficiently with the thumbs to allow each ring to be eased from its groove and lifted clear of the piston. This is a very delicate operation necessitating great care. Piston rings are very brittle and will break easily. An alternative method of removing piston rings safely especially when the rings are gummed up, is shown in the accompanying illustration. Use three narrow strips of tin cut from an old oil can, slipped between the rings and the piston.

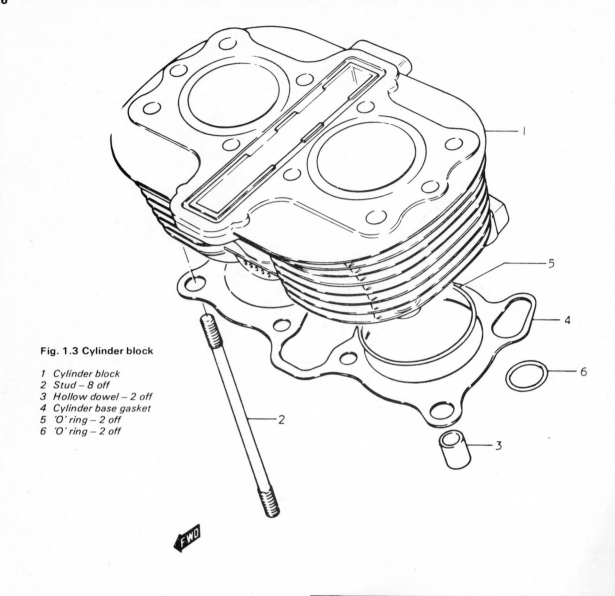

Fig. 1.3 Cylinder block

1 Cylinder block
2 Stud – 8 off
3 Hollow dowel – 2 off
4 Cylinder base gasket
5 'O' ring – 2 off
6 'O' ring – 2 off

FWD

Fig. 1.4 Freeing gummed rings

7.2 Securing cam chain by length of wire when lifting head

8 Dismantling the engine/gearbox: removing the gear indicator switch, starter motor and alternator

1   Remove the two screws securing the gear indicator switch to the gearbox wall and lift the switch away, together with the sealing ring. The switch contact and spring should be displaced from the end of the gear change drum and stored in a safe place.

2   Slacken evenly and remove the screws retaining the alternator cover in place. Remove the cover and gasket and displace the single locating dowel to avoid loss. The alternator cover serves as a mounting for the alternator stator and should be stored accordingly to avoid accidental damage to the coils. To gain access to the starter motor remove the chrome cover which is held by two screws. The starter motor is secured by two bolts passing through a flange in the end cap, into the crankcase. Remove the screws and ease the starter motor across towards the right-hand side until it hits the chamber wall. The motor can then be lifted up at the right-hand end and away from the engine. If difficulty is encountered in moving the starter motor initially, a wooden lever may be used between the gear casing wall and starter motor front cover. **NEVER** strike the starter motor shaft as this may damage the reduction gear within the motor.

3   Withdraw the starter motor idler gear together with the gear spindle and two thrust washers.

4   Remove the bolt retaining the alternator rotor. The rotor centre boss is provided with two milled flats to which a spanner may be fitted to prevent rotor rotation during bolt removal. The alternator rotor is a tapered fit on the crankshaft end, and as such must be drawn from position. The centre of the rotor has an internal thread provided to take a slide hammer. This tool consists of a long, headed rod upon which a free sliding weight is fitted. After screwing the rod firmly into the rotor centre the weight is slid along the rod with force until it strikes the head. This action will separate the two tapers. If a suitable slide hammer is not available, the pivot bolt which supports the machine's swinging arm may be used together with any suitable weight of approximately $\frac{1}{2}$ lb. Check the thread compatibility before removing the swinging arm pivot shaft

5   On removal of the rotor, the starter motor driven sprocket and its two needle roller bearings and bronze thrust washer may be withdrawn from the shaft.

9 Dismantling the engine/gearbox: removing the contact breaker plate and the automatic timing unit

1   Remove the contact breaker cover plate if this has not already been done. The contact breaker plate is retained by three screws through elongated holes, which allow a small amount of timing adjustment. Before loosening the screws and removing the plate, mark the plate and the top screw boss with a punch to allow easy and accurate timing on replacement. Ensure that the two punch marks are placed accurately adjacent to each other. Remove the contact breaker plate and pull the wiring through from the tunnel in the primary drive casing.

2   The automatic timing unit is retained by a single bolt in the end of the crankshaft. With a 17 mm spanner holding the crankshaft rotation bolt, the ATU bolt can be loosened easily and the unit pulled from place.

10 Dismantling the engine/gearbox: removing the primary drive cover, dismantling the clutch and primary drive pinion

1   Slacken the primary drive casing screws evenly, in a diagonal sequence, and remove them. Note the single screw which is located within the contact breaker housing chamber, to the left of the crankshaft oil seal. Remove the casing and gaskets.

2   Unscrew the six clutch spring bolts a little at a time to

maintain equal pressure on the pressure plate, and then remove them together with the washers and springs. Withdraw the pressure plate. The clutch plate may be removed singly or as a complete sandwich. Note the sequence of plates to aid subsequent reassembly. The innermost plain plate is slightly thicker than the remaining plates. To aid identification all but the inner plate are marked with a small 'O'. Withdraw the clutch thrust piece complete with the thrust bearing and two thrust washers and then pull out the clutch pushrod.

3   To enable removal of the clutch centre boss and outer drum, the centre nut must be unscrewed after bending down the tab washer. To prevent rotation of the clutch when loosening the nut, first refit the gear change lever and the gearbox sprocket. Place the engine in top gear. The sprocket can now be held steady by inserting a large screwdriver across one tooth so that it locates with one of the bolt lugs on the face of the gearbox wall. This operation requires the help of an assistant. It is imperative that the screwdriver is held firmly; slippage will almost certainly damage the cases.

4   Remove the centre nut and tab washer and withdraw the clutch centre boss followed by the heavy washer. Remove the outer drum and final washer in a similar manner.

5   To remove the primary drive pinion bolt it is necessary to stop the engine from rotating. This is best achieved by placing a close fitting metal bar through one or both small end eyes and allowing the bar to bear down on small wooden blocks placed across the crankcase mouth. On no account must the bar be allowed to bear directly onto the gasket face. Having stopped the engine from rotating remove the gear retaining bolt. The primary drive pinion is a parallel fit on the crankshaft, located by a large Woodruff key. Slide the pinion off the shaft and prise out the key. If difficulty is encountered in removing the pinion, two levers may be inserted between the rear face of the pinion and the crankcase wall. Levers used for this purpose must be wielded with great care, to prevent damage to the aluminium castings.

11 Dismantling the engine/gearbox: removing the gearchange mechanism

1   Slacken the pivot screw, which passes through the gear change drum stopper arm, sufficiently to allow the arm to be lifted up away from the change drum and released so that roller end clears the end of the drum. The pivot bolt may now be unscrewed fully without danger of the return spring tearing the bolt out of the last few threads in the casing. Detach the return spring from the anchor plate in the casing in order to free the arm fully.

2   Depress the main change arm so that the pawls clear the change drum end and then withdraw the gearchange shaft complete with the arm.

3   Remove from the roof of the gearbox, the change drum detent bolt, spring and plunger.

4   Free the change drum guide plate by removing the final bolt.

12 Dismantling the engine/gearbox: removing the oil pump and kickstart return spring

1   Remove the three screws which secure the oil pump to the wall of the primary drive casing. Lift the oil pump away complete with the drive pinion. Note the two oilway O-rings which rest in the recesses in the casing. The oil pump should be placed to one side for dismantling and examination at a later stage.

2   Grasp the outer turned end of the kickstart return spring with a stout pair of pliers. Pull the spring end from the anchor hole in the casing and allow it to unwind in an anti-clockwise direction in a controlled manner. Prise the spring guide from the centre of the spring and then displace the spring inner thread end from the radially drilled hole in the kickstart shaft. Draw the spring from the shaft.

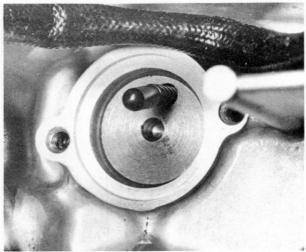
8.1 Do not lose gear indicator switch contact or spring

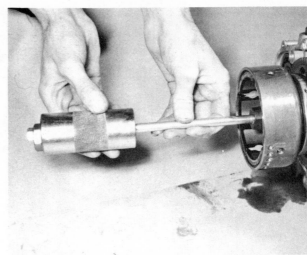
8.4 Use slide hammer to detach alternator rotor

9.1 Mark clearly the stator plate before removal

10.1 Note hidden screw when removing the primary drive cover

11.1 Slacken stopper arm bolt to allow roller to clear change drum end

12.2 Release kickstart spring tension in anti-clockwise direction

3   No further dismantling of the kickstart is possible until after separation of the crankcases.

13 Dismantling the engine/gearbox: removing the oil filter

1   Invert the engine so that it is resting on the cylinder head holding down studs and the rear of the gearbox casing. Two circular covers are fitted to the base of the crankcase. The rear cover encloses the oil filter element. The front plate covers the oil pick-up strainer gauze. This need not be disturbed at this juncture as the strainer may be removed after crankcase separation, complete with the pick-up funnel.
2   Remove the three domed nuts securing the oil filter cover. The cover is under pressure from the oil filter locating spring; be prepared for it to fly off, followed closely by the spring. Lift out, and discard the oil filter element.

14 Dismantling the engine/gearbox: separating the crankcase halves

1   From the wall of the primary drive chamber, remove the bearing retainer plate which is secured by three countersunk screws. These screws are often very tight; take care not to damage their heads. A similar plate is fitted to the gearbox left-hand wall, secured by three bolts. Bend down the tabbed edges of the plate to free the nuts.
2   Slacken evenly and remove the crankcase upper half securing bolts, after repositioning the engine to gain access. Remove also the single nut from the stud forward of the gearbox output shaft, in the gearbox wall. Invert the engine again so that it is resting on the cylinder holding studs and the rear edge of the upper casing. Loosen evenly and remove the 6 mm and 8 mm securing bolts. Each 8 mm bolt is identified by a number stamped on an adjoining portion of the casing. To prevent stress in the casings, these bolts should be slackened in sequence, commencing with the highest number and continuing through to the lowest number.
3   Crankcase separation is carried out with the engine inverted so that the lower half may be lifted away leaving all major components in the upper half.
4   Separation of the crankcase halves should be carried out with care, using a rawhide mallet initially, to release the two cases from the gasket compound which was used on original assembly. **DO NOT** use levers placed between the two mating surfaces in an effort to hasten separation. Treatment of this nature will almost certainly damage the machined surfaces, causing subsequent oil leakage.
5   After separation, study the internal components carefully before continuing with the dismantling operation. This will help

prevent confusion when reassembly is being carried out. Note and remove the O-ring which seats in a recess in the upper casing. Check the two location dowels for tightness. If loose, they should be removed, to avoid loss.

15 Dismantling the engine/gearbox: removing the balance shaft, crankshaft and gear shafts

1   Lift the balance shaft out of position, rotating it at the same time so that the driven gear clears the drive gear on the crank-shaft. Grasp the crankshaft with both hands and lift it upwards out of the casing, as a complete unit, together with the oil seals and the cam chain. If the crankshaft is firmly seated, use a rawhide mallet to free it from the casing. Use great care when using this procedure. Note the main bearing outer race location pins in the upper crankcase half. If they are loose, remove them with a pair of pliers.
2   Lift out the two gearbox shafts individually, complete with pinions and seals. Note the positions of the bearing location half clips, which prevent axial movement, and prise them from position. The two shaft assemblies should be put to one side for further attention at a later stage.

14.1 Separate lower casing from upper casing

15.1a Lift out the layshaft followed by ...

15.1b ... the mainshaft, both as complete units

15.1c Likewise remove balance shaft and crankshaft

Fig. 1.5 Crankshaft assembly – component parts

1 Crankshaft assembly
2 Connecting rod – 2 off
3 Thrust washer – 2 off
4 Thrust washer – 2 off
5 Big-end bearing – 2 off
6 RH flywheel/mainshaft
7 RH flywheel
8 LH flywheel/mainshaft
9 LH flywheel
10 Camsprocket shaft
11 Main bearing
12 Main bearing – 3 off
13 Circlip
14 Balance shaft drive pinion
15 Drive pin
16 Bearing half clip
17 RH oil seal
18 Dowel pin – 3 off
19 Oil seal
20 Piston – 2 off
21 Piston ring set – 2 off
22 Gudgeon pin – 2 off
23 Circlip – 4 off
24 Primary drive pinion
25 Nut
26 Concave washer
27 Woodruff key

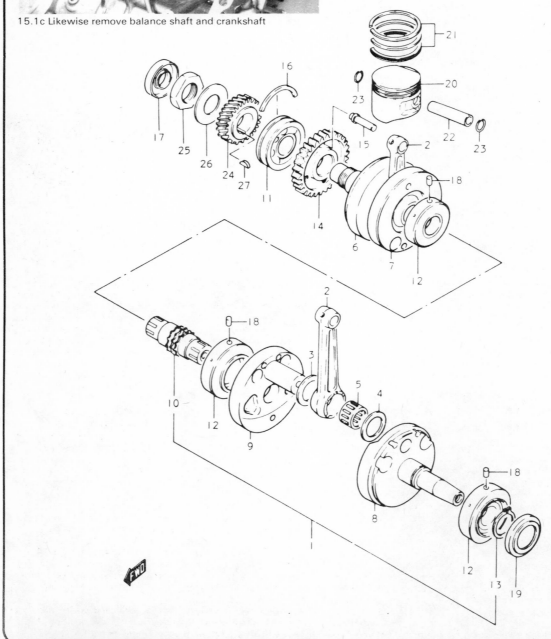

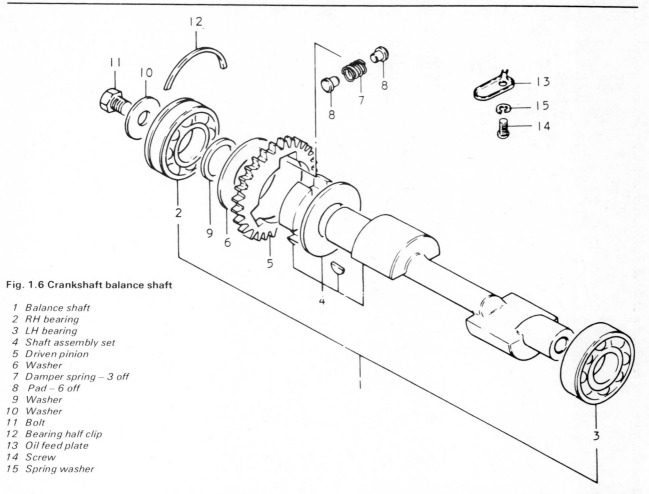

Fig. 1.6 Crankshaft balance shaft

1 Balance shaft
2 RH bearing
3 LH bearing
4 Shaft assembly set
5 Driven pinion
6 Washer
7 Damper spring – 3 off
8 Pad – 6 off
9 Washer
10 Washer
11 Bolt
12 Bearing half clip
13 Oil feed plate
14 Screw
15 Spring washer

16 Dismantling the engine/gearbox: removing the gear selector mechanism

1 Remove the single screw which locates the selector fork rod in place. Withdraw the rod towards the right-hand side and lift out the three freed selector forks. Replace the forks on the rod in their original positions to facilitate subsequent assembly.
2 The gear change drum is now free to be pulled from place in the casing.
3 The crankcase upper half now contains only the cam chain tensioner blade. This may be detached, if required, by removing the single securing nut from the forward edge of the chain tunnel.

17 Dismantling the engine/gearbox: removing the kickstart assembly, oil pick-up funnel and baffle plates

1 If damage to the kickstart mechanism is suspected, the assembly should be removed from the crankcase lower half as follows: Detach the kickstart pawl plate from the inside of the gearbox chamber by removing the two countersunk screws. Displace the circlip from the outer end of the kickstart shaft and then remove the three countersunk screws from the flanged shaft bush. After withdrawing the boss from the casing, the kickstart shaft assembly may be manoeuvred from position in the opposite direction. Place the complete assembly to one side for examination at a later stage.
2 The oil pick-up funnel is secured to the crankcase half by three screws and is sealed by an O-ring interposed between the

mating surfaces. Removal of the funnel itself is not strictly necessary except as an aid to oil passage cleaning. The oil pick-up strainer gauze should be removed for cleaning as a matter of course. To remove the screen, unscrew the two retaining bolts and twist the unit to the left. It will be seen on removal that the rear edge of the screen, which is obscured by the crankcase, is located by a turned tag.
3 Removal of the baffle plates fitted within the lower casing is not necessary unless the engine is badly gummed-up with oil. Detaching the plates will improve access for cleaning.

18 Examination and renovation: general

1 Before examining the component parts of the dismantled engine/gearbox unit for wear, it is essential that they should be cleaned thoroughly. Use a paraffin/petrol mix to remove all traces of oil and sludge which may have accumulated within the engine.
2 Examine the crankcase castings for cracks or other signs of damage. If a crack is discovered, it will require professional attention or in an extreme case, renewal of the casting.
3 Examine carefully each part to determine the extent of wear. If in doubt, check with the tolerance figures whenever they are given in the specifications at the beginning of the Chapter or in the text. The following sections will indicate what type of wear can be expected and in many cases, the acceptable limits.
4 Use clean, lint-free rag for cleaning and drying the various components, otherwise there is risk of small particles obstructing the internal oilways.

19 Examination and replacement: crankshaft assembly

1 The crankshaft assembly comprises two separate sets of flywheels with their respective big-ends, connecting rods and main bearings, pressed together to form a single unit.
2 In the event of main bearing failure, it is beyond the means of the average owner to separate the flywheel assemblies and to realign them to the high standard of accuracy required. In consequence, the complete crankshaft assembly must be taken to a Suzuki Service Agent for the necessary repairs and renovation, or exchanged for a fully reconditioned unit.
3 Main bearing failure will be immediately obvious when the bearings are inspected after the old oil has been washed out. If any play is evident or if the bearings do not run freely, renewal is essential. The rollers and bearing tracks of the three roller type main bearings may be inspected visually by moving the outer race of each to one side. Scoring, flaking and pitting of either the tracks or the rollers indicates the need for renewal. Warning of main bearing failure is usually given by a characteristic rumble that can be readily heard when the engine is running. Some vibration will also be felt, which is transmitted via the footrests.
4 Big-end failure is characterised by a pronounced knock that will be most noticeable when the engine is working hard. There should be no play whatsoever in either of the connecting rods, when they are pushed and pulled in a vertical direction. Wear of the big-ends may be assessed by measuring the deflection of each connecting rod in line with the crankshaft at the small end eye. Play of more than 3.0 mm (0.12 in) indicates bearing wear. Check also the axial float at each big-end by inserting a feeler gauge between one big-end eye face and the adjacent thrust washer. The recommended limit is 1.0 mm (0.04 in).

20 Examination and renovation: connecting rods

1 Bending of either connecting rod during normal usage is unlikely, unless an unusual occurrence, such as a dropped valve, has caused the engine to lock. Carelessness when removing a tight gudgeon pin can also give rise to a similar problem. It is not advisable to straighten a bent connecting rod but as rods are not supplied separately a complete crankshaft assembly must be acquired.
2 The small end eye of the connecting rod is unbushed and as such it will be necessary to renew the connecting rod if the gudgeon pin is a slack fit. Always check the oil holes in the small end eye are not blocked. If the oil supply is cut off, the bearing surfaces will wear very rapidly.

21 Examination and renovation: balance shaft

1 The balance shaft runs on two journal ball bearings which may be checked in a similar manner to that described for crankshaft main bearings. These bearings are of ample proportions for the small loadings involved and should therefore have a long service life.
2 Inspect the condition of the shaft pinion and also the drive pinion on the crankshaft with which it meshes. Examine for excessive wear and broken or chipped teeth. Renewal of the drive pinion on the crankshaft should be entrusted to a Suzuki Service Agent who will have the necessary equipment to press the pinion and bearing from place.
3 Grasp the balance shaft pinion firmly and attempt to turn it whilst holding the shaft steady. If looseness or rattling of the three shock absorber springs can be detected, the balance shaft should be dismantled and the springs removed.
4 The balance shaft right-hand bearing and the pinion may be pulled from place using a two or three-legged sprocket puller. Loosen the centre bolt approximately two turns. Leave the bolt in place as a thrust point for the puller centre. Draw the pinion off slowly, bringing with it the bearing, undoing the centre bolt at intervals to give room for movement. To prevent the three

shock absorber springs from flying out in an uncontrolled manner, wrap a rag around the assembly until the pinion and bearing have been removed. Any springs then remaining in place may be prised from position. Note the pads placed at both ends of each spring. The shock absorber centre boss is a tight interference fit on the shaft, located by a Woodruff key. Removal is not required. If the boss becomes worn it must be renewed complete with the shaft. These components are not supplied separately.
5 Reassembly of the shock absorber unit is as follows: Place each spring and set of pads in position in the recessed centre boss. Position the pinion and push it fully home onto the springs. Note that a punch mark is provided on the outer face of the pinion. This punch mark must be aligned with a similar mark on the centre boss face. Replace the bearing, ensuring that it is fitted with the circlip retaining groove outermost. Fit and tighten the centre bolt and washer.
6 The balance shaft left-hand bearing is a tight fit on the shaft and may be drawn from place by using a sprocket puller. When refitting the bearing, it must be placed with the projecting pin towards the inside.

22 Examination and replacement: oil seals

1 An oil seal is fitted to the left-hand end of the crankshaft to prevent oil loss into the alternator chamber. A second crankshaft seal is fitted within the primary drive cover which prevents oil from reaching the contact breaker assembly. The gearbox utilises three seals; one at the mainshaft left-hand end and two in line on the layshaft left-hand end. If a seal is damaged or has shown a tendency to leak, it must be renewed.
2 Oil seals also tend to lose their effectiveness if they harden with age. It is difficult to give any firm recommendation in this respect except to say that if there is any doubt about the condition of a seal, renew it as a precaution.

23 Cylinder block: examination and renovation

1 The usual indication of badly worn cylinder bores and pistons is excessive smoking from the exhausts and piston slap, a metallic rattle that occurs when there is little or no load on the engine. If the top of the bore of the cylinder block is examined carefully, it will be found that there is a ridge on the thrust side, the depth of which will vary according to the rate of wear that has taken place. This marks the limit of travel of the uppermost piston ring.
2 Measure the bore diameter just below the ridge. Take two measurements, at 90° to one another. Take two similar measurements half way down the bore and at a position just above the lower edge of the bore. If any measurement exceeds the maximum allowable, the cylinder should be rebored and fitted with an oversize piston. If the difference between the maximum and minimum measurement exceeds 1.0 mm (0.039 in) a rebore is also required.
3 If an internal micrometer is not available, the amount of cylinder bore wear can be measured by inserting the piston without rings so that it is approximately $\frac{3}{4}$ inch from the top of the bore. If it is possible to insert a 0.060 mm (0.0024 in) feeler gauge between the piston and the cylinder wall on the thrust side of the piston, remedial action must be taken.
4 Oversize pistons are available in two sizes; + 0.5 mm (0.020 in) and + 1.0 mm (0.040 in).
5 Check that the surface of the cylinder bores is free from score marks or other damage that may have resulted from an earlier engine seizure or a displaced gudgeon pin. A rebore will be necessary to remove any deep scores, irrespective of the amount of bore wear that has taken place, otherwise a compression leak will occur.
6 Make sure the external cooling fins of the cylinder block are not clogged with oil or road dirt, which will prevent the free flow of air and cause the engine to overheat.

19.3 Move outer races to one side to inspect the main bearings

21.4 Balance shaft centre boss is located by a Woodruff key

21.5a When refitting shaft pinion ensure punch marks align

21.5b Replace backing plate and washer and ...

21.5c ... bearing which is a tight interference fit

21.5d Secure bearing by means of the bolt and washer

24 Examination and renovation: pistons and piston rings

1   Attention to the pistons and piston rings can be overlooked if a rebore is necessary, since new components will be fitted.
2   If a rebore is not considered necessary, examine each piston closely. Reject pistons that are scored or badly discoloured as the result of exhaust gases by-passing the rings.
3   Remove all carbon from the piston crowns, using a blunt scraper, which will not damage the surface of the piston. Clean away all carbon deposits from the valve cutaways and finish off with metal polish so that a clean, shining surface is achieved. Carbon will not adhere so readily to a polished surface. Using an external micrometer or vernier gauge, measure the external diameter of each piston across the thrust faces (at 90° to the gudgeon pin line), at the bottom of the skirt. Take a second measurement approximately 15 mm (0·590 in) up from the lower edge of the skirt. If either measurement exceeds that given for the service limit, the piston is in need of renewal.
4   Check that the gudgeon pin bosses are not worn or the circlip grooves damaged. Check that the piston ring grooves are not enlarged. Side float should not exceed 0·18 mm (0·007 in) for the top ring and second ring, and 0·15 mm (0·006 in) for the oil control ring.
5   Piston ring wear can be measured by inserting the rings in the bore from the top, pushing them down with the base of the piston so that they are square in the bore and about 1½ inches down. If the end gap exceeds 0·6 mm (0·024 in) on any of the rings, renewal is necessary. A replacement set of rings is comparatively inexpensive and it is considered good practice to renew them as a matter of course whenever the engine is dismantled.
6   Check that there is no build up of carbon on the inside surface of the rings or in the grooves of the pistons. Any build-up should be removed by careful scraping.
7   The piston crowns will show whether the engine has been rebored on some previous occasion. All oversize pistons have the rebore size stamped on the crown. This information is essential when ordering replacement piston rings.
8   If new piston rings are fitted but a rebore has not taken place, the cylinder bores should be 'glaze busted'. This honing operation, as the name suggests, removes the highly polished glazed surface of the bore which has been caused by the countless up and down strokes of the piston and rings. If 'glaze busting' is not carried out, the time required to run-in the new rings will be greatly extended.

25 Examination and renovation: cylinder head and valves

1   Remove the cam followers and adjuster shims from the cylinder head, marking each follower so that it may be refitted in its original location. It is best to remove all carbon deposits from the combustion chambers before removing the valves for inspection and grinding-in. Use a blunt end chisel or scraper so that the surfaces are not damaged. Finish off with a metal polish to achieve a smooth, shining surface. If a mirror finish is required, a high speed felt mop and polishing soap may be used. A chuck attached to a flexible drive will facilitate the polishing operation.
2   A valve spring compression tool must be used to compress each set of valve springs in turn, thereby allowing the split collets to be removed from the valve cap and the valve springs and caps to be freed. Keep each set of parts separate and mark each valve so that it can be replaced in the correct combustion chamber. There is no danger of inadvertently replacing an inlet valve in an exhaust position, or vice-versa, as the valve heads are of different sizes. The normal method of marking valves for later identification is by centre punching them on the valve head. This method is not recommended on valves, or any other highly stressed components, as it will produce high stress points and may lead to early failure. Tie-on labels, suitably inscribed, are ideal for the purpose.

3   Before giving the valve and valve seats further attention, check the clearance between each valve stem and the guide in which it operates. Clearances are as follows:

Standard	Service Limit
Inlet valve/guide clearance	
0.02 - 0.05 mm	0.09 mm
(0.0008 - 0.0020 in)	(0.0035 in)
Exhaust valve/guide clearance	
0.03 - 0.06 mm	0.10 mm
(0.0012 - 0.0024 in)	(0.0039 in)

Measure the valve stem at the point of greatest wear and then measure again at right-angles to the first measurement. If the valve stem is below the service limit it must be renewed.

Standard	Service Limit
Inlet valve stem	
6.965 - 6.980 mm	6.90 mm
(0.2742 - 0.2748 in)	(0.2717 in)
Exhaust valve stem	
6.955 - 6.970 mm	6.805 mm
(0.2738 - 0.2744 in)	(0.2679 in)

The valve stem/guide clearance can be measured with the use of a dial gauge and a new valve. Place the new valve into the guide and measure the amount of shake with the dial guage tip resting against the top of the stem. If the amount of wear is greater than the wear limit, the guide must be renewed.
4   To remove the old valve guide, place the cylinder head in an oven and heat it to about 150°C. The old guide can now be tapped out from the cylinder side. To prevent distortion of the large alloy casting it is essential that the cylinder head is heated evenly. For this reason an oven **must** be used in preference to a blow torch or other methods of heating. If inexperienced in this type of work, the advice of a Suzuki Service Agent should be sought. Before drifting a guide from place, remove any carbon deposits which may have built up on the guide end projecting into the port. Carbon deposits will impede the progress of the guide and may damage the cylinder head.
     If possible, use a double diameter drift. The smaller diameter should be close to that of the valve stem, and the larger diameter slightly smaller than that of valve guide. Provided that care is exercised, a parallel shanked drift may be used as a substitute.
5   Valve grinding is a simple task. Commence by smearing a trace of fine valve grinding compound (carborundum paste) on the valve seat and apply a suction tool to the head of the valve. Oil the valve stem and insert the valve in the guide so that the two surfaces to be ground in make contact with one another. With a semi-rotary motion, grind in the valve head to the seat, using a backward and forward action. Lift the valve occasionally so that the grinding compound is distributed evenly. Repeat the application until an unbroken ring of light grey matt finish is obtained on both valve and seat. This denotes the grinding operation is now complete. Before passing to the next valve, make sure that all traces of the valve grinding compound have been removed from both the valve and its seat and that none has entered the valve guide. If this precaution is not observed, rapid wear will take place due to the highly abrasive nature of the carborundum base.
6   If, after grinding, it is found that the width of the grey seating ring is greater than 1·5 mm (0·06 in) the valve seat must be recut using a special cutting tool. Angles of 75° and 15° must be cut in order to reduce the valve seat width, followed by a 45° cut in order to restore the correct seat angle and the correct seat width to within the range 1·0 – 1·2 mm (0·04 – 0·05 in). Because of the expense of purchasing the three seat cutters and because of the accuracy with which cutting must be carried out, it is strongly recommended that the cylinder head be returned to a Suzuki Service Agent for attention.
     It follows that when material is removed from the valve

seat, the valve stem will protrude further from the upper side of the cylinder head. In extreme cases it may be found that on adjustment of the cam clearances, the prescribed clearance cannot be arrived at even with the thinnest adjustment shim available. If this is found to be the case, removal of a small amount of metal from the valve stem end is permissible. Grinding should be carried out on a suitable machine so that the stem end remains square with the shank. Where grinding to attain the correct clearance reduces the distance between the top of the stem and the upper edge of the collet groove to less than 4·00 mm (0·1574 in) a new valve seat insert must be fitted. This operation is highly skilled requiring the use of very specialised equipment.

7 Where deep pitting of the seat and valve is encountered, the seat should be recut as previously described. The valve face may be ground back on a special grinding machine to an angle of 45°, provided that after grinding, the depth of the valve periphery has not been reduced to less than 1·5 mm (0·06 in).

8 Examine the condition of the valve collets and the groove on the valve stem in which they seat. If there is any sign of damage, new parts should be fitted. Check that the valve spring collar is not cracked. If the collets work loose or the collar splits whilst the engine is running, a valve could drop into the cylinder and cause extensive damage.

9 Check the free length of each of the valve springs. The springs have reached their serviceable limit when they have compressed to the limit readings given in the Specifications Section of this Chapter.

10 Reassemble the valve and valve springs by reversing the dismantling procedure. Ensure that all the springs are fitted with the close coils downwards towards the cylinder head. Fit new oil seals to each inlet valve guide and oil both the valve stem and the valve guide, prior to reassembly. Take special care to ensure the valve guide oil seal is not damaged when the valve is inserted. As a final check after assembly, give the end of each valve stem a light tap with a hammer, to make sure the split collets have located correctly.

11 Check the cylinder head for straightness, especially if it has shown a tendency to leak oil at the cylinder head joint. If there is any evidence of warpage, provided it is not too great, the cylinder head must be either machined flat or a new head fitted. Most cases of cylinder head warpage can be traced to unequal tensioning of the cylinder head nuts and bolts by tightening them in incorrect sequence.

25.10a Fit new oil seals to both inlet valve guides

25.10b Lubricate valve stems thoroughly before insertion

25.10c Replace spring seat and valve springs

25.10d Install collets after compressing springs

26 Examination and renovation: camshafts, cam followers and camshaft drive sprockets

1   Inspect the cams for signs of wear such as scored lobes, scuffing, or indentation. The cams should have a smooth surface. The complete camshaft must be replaced if any lobes are worn or indented, through lubrication failure etc. In due course even normal wear of each cam lobe may progress to the stage where full valve lift is no longer possible. Measure each cam from the lobe to the base circle, comparing the overall height with these figures.

Minimum cam height

	400 and 400B	**400C**
Inlet	*36.15 mm*	*36.37 mm*
	(1.4232 in)	*(1.4319 in)*
Exhaust	*35.60 mm*	*35.95 mm*
	(1.4016 in)	*(1.4154 in)*

If any one cam on either camshaft is below the minimum figure, that camshaft should be renewed in order to restore performance.

2   Refit both camshafts in the cylinder head and fit the bearing caps and bolts. Tighten the bolts to a torque wrench setting of 0·8 – 1·2 kg m (6 – 8 ft lb). Check the clearance between the camshaft journals and the bearing surfaces. This is most easily accomplished by fitting a dial gauge to the cylinder head and moving the camshaft in a vertical or horizontal plane. If the clearances exceed those figures given in the specifications, remove the camshafts, refit the bearing caps and check the diameter of each bearing, to determine whether the camshaft or cam bearing is at fault.

3   If it is found that the camshaft bearings are worn or badly scored, the cylinder head and bearing caps must be renewed. There is no provision for renewing the bearings as the camshafts run directly in the cylinder head material.

4   Examine the camshaft chain sprockets for hooked, worn, or broken teeth. If any damage is found, the camshaft sprocket in question should be renewed. Each sprocket is retained on the camshaft flange by two socket screws. When refitting either sprocket note that each is marked IN or EX as are the camshafts. It is important that the sprockets are fitted on the correct camshaft and in the position shown in the accompanying illustration. Incorrect assembly will prevent accurate valve timing. Apply a small quantity of locking fluid to the securing screws during reassembly.

5   The camshaft drive sprocket is an integral part of the crankshaft and therefore if damage is evident, the crankshaft must be renewed. Fortunately, this drastic course of action is rarely necessary since the parts concerned are fully enclosed and well lubricated, working under ideal conditions.

6   Inspect the external surfaces of the cam followers for signs of scoring or fracture. If damage is evident, the component must be renewed. If scoring has occurred it follows that similar damage may be found in the appropriate guide tunnel in the cylinder head. Damage to the tunnels cannot be rectified under normal circumstances and therefore a new cylinder head must be obtained. Insert each cam follower into the guide tunnel from which it was removed. Only the lightest pressure should be used to insert each follower. If a follower is inserted even at a slight angle, binding against the tunnel will result. Any effort made to tap the follower in will almost certainly jam the follower solidly. Removal is then very difficult!

Check the clearance between each cam follower and guide tunnel. Unfortunately, no precise figures are available but the follower should be a good sliding fit, with no perceptible play from side to side. Excess play will allow the cam follower to tilt, causing noisy operation and accelerated wear of the cylinder head.

27 Examination and renovation: cam chain and chain tensioner mechanism

1   Inspect the cam chain for obvious signs of damage, such as broken or missing rollers or fractured links. Some indication of the amount of chain wear may be gained by checking the extent of adjustment remaining on the automatic tensioner assembly. If the plunger has moved towards the end of the stroke, it may be assumed that the chain is near the end of its useful life. Wear of the chain can be measured by washing it in petrol, then compressing it endwise so that the free play in both runs is taken up fully. Anchor one end, then pull on the chain so that it stretches as far as possible. If the extension measured exceeds $\frac{1}{4}$ inch per foot, the chain must be renewed. Although the cam chain works in almost ideal conditions, being fully lubricated and enclosed, wear will develop after an extended mileage. If there is any doubt as to the chain's condition, it should be renewed, as breakage will cause extensive engine damage.

2   Loosen the locking screw on the chain tensioner body to free the plunger pushrod. Rotate the adjuster knob anticlockwise so that the plunger may be pushed in fully, and check that the plunger moves in and out freely, without any tendency to bind. If plunger movement is not perfectly smooth, the complete unit should be renewed.

3   Inspect the surfaces of the two chain guide blades. If the rubber has been badly scored by the chain or is coming away from the steel backing, the blade in question should be renewed. A jockey sprocket is fitted between the two camshafts. Clean the sprocket and carrier assembly thoroughly in petrol and check that the sprocket rotates freely. Inspect the sprocket teeth using criteria for renewal as given for the camshaft sprockets.

28 Examination and renovation: tachometer drive assembly

1   The worm drive to the tachometer is an integral part of the exhaust camshaft which meshes with a pinion attached to the cylinder head cover. If the worm is damaged or badly worn, it will be necessary to renew the camshaft complete.

2   The driveshaft and pinion are a single part retained in the cylinder head in a bush housing which is secured by a plate and screw. Renewal is therefore straightforward. It is unlikely that wear will develop on either the drive or driven pinion as both are well lubricated and lightly loaded.

28.2 Tachometer drive housing is held by plate and screw

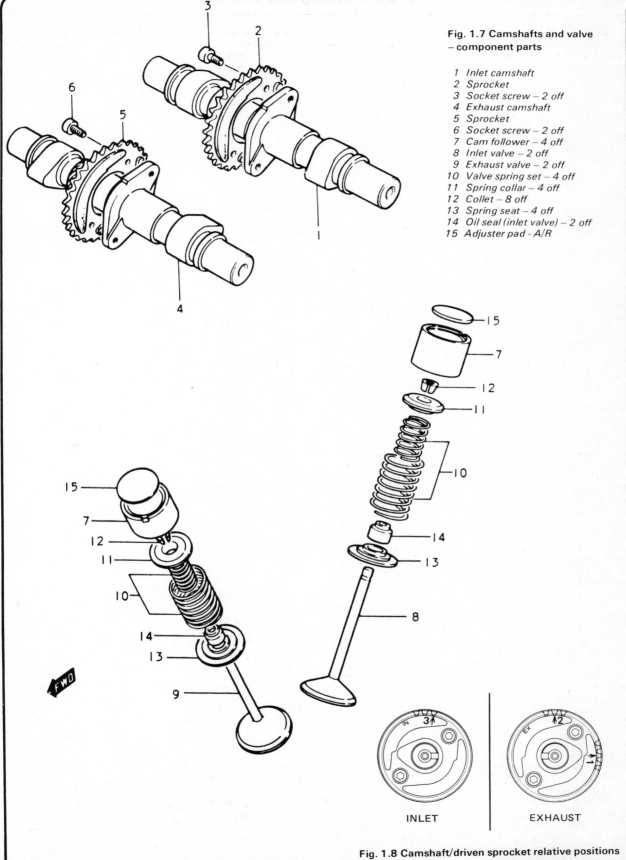

**Fig. 1.7 Camshafts and valve
– component parts**

1 Inlet camshaft
2 Sprocket
3 Socket screw – 2 off
4 Exhaust camshaft
5 Sprocket
6 Socket screw – 2 off
7 Cam follower – 4 off
8 Inlet valve – 2 off
9 Exhaust valve – 2 off
10 Valve spring set – 4 off
11 Spring collar – 4 off
12 Collet – 8 off
13 Spring seat – 4 off
14 Oil seal (inlet valve) – 2 off
15 Adjuster pad - A/R

INLET

EXHAUST

Fig. 1.8 Camshaft/driven sprocket relative positions

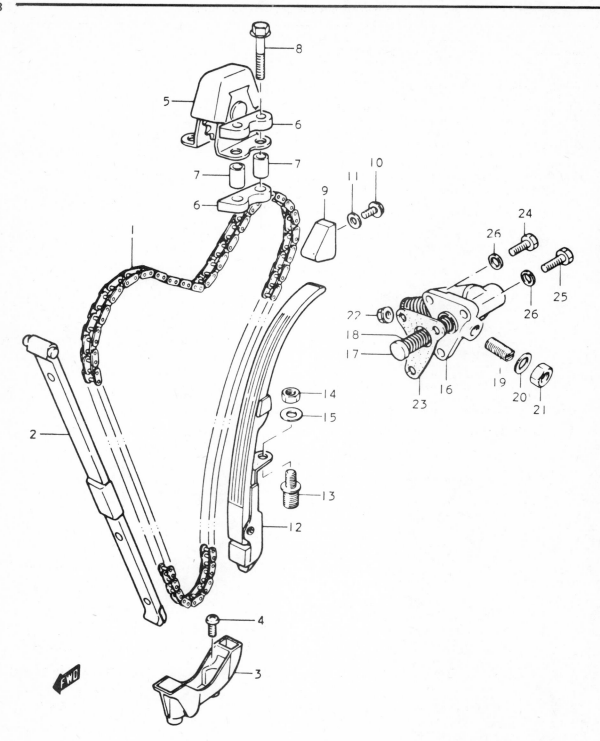

Fig. 1.9 Cam chain and tensioner assembly

1 Camshaft drive chain	8 Bolt – 4 off	15 Washer	21 Nut
2 Chain guide blade	9 Chain guide block	16 Chain tensioner assembly	22 Nut
3 Blade seat	10 Bolt	17 Plunger	23 Gasket
4 Screw – 2 off	11 Washer	18 Spring	24 Bolt – 2 off
5 Jockey sprocket	12 Chain tensioner blade	19 Locking screw	25 Bolt
6 Damper block – 4 off	13 Stud	20 Washer	26 Washer – 3 off
7 Collar – 4 off	14 Nut		

29 Examination and renovation: gearbox components

1   It should not be necessary to dismantle either of the gear clusters unless damage has occurred to any of the pinions or if the caged needle roller bearings require attention.

2   The accompanying illustration shows how both clusters of the gearbox are assembled on their respective shafts. It is imperative that the gear clusters, including the thrust washers, are assembled in EXACTLY the correct sequence, otherwise constant gear selection problems will occur.

In order to eliminate the risk of misplacement, make rough sketches as the clusters are dismantled. Also strip and rebuild as soon as possible, to reduce any confusion which might occur at a later date.

3   When dismantling the gear shafts, the journal ball bearings may be pulled from position, using a standard two or three-legged sprocket puller. A special locking washer is fitted to the layshaft between two adjacent gear pinions. The washer is placed between the 3rd gear and 4th gear pinions. To free the washer, and release the next washer in the sequence, it must be turned slightly so that the internal serrations clear the shaft splines. The washer may then be pulled from place. Similarly, on reassembly, the washer should be turned so that it engages correctly.

3   The 2nd gear pinion on the mainshaft is an interference fit and will require pulling from position. On refitting this pinion, it is essential that it is so placed that the distance between its outer face and that of the 1st gear pinion is 114·7 (4·516 in). This measurement is critical for correct rotational clearance and perfect alignment. Before refitting the pinion, treat the inner box with a high shear strength locking compound. Suzuki recommend the use of Thread Lock Super 103K.

After refitting the 2nd gear pinion, check that the 6th gear pinion is free to rotate and has not become locked by migrating locking fluid.

4   Give the gearbox components a close visual inspection for signs of wear or damage such as broken or chipped teeth, worn dogs, damaged or worn splines and bent selectors. Replace any parts found unserviceable because they cannot be reclaimed in a satisfactory manner.

5   The gearbox bearings must be free from play and show no signs of roughness when they are rotated. After thorough washing in petrol the bearings should be examined for roughness and play. Also check for pitting on the roller tracks.

6   It is advisable to renew the gearbox oil seals irrespective of their condition. Should a re-used oil seal fail at a later date, a considerable amount of work is involved to gain access to renew it.

7   Check the gear selector rod for straightness by rolling it on a sheet of plate glass. A bent rod will cause difficulty in selecting gears and will make the gear change particularly heavy.

8   The selector forks should be examined closely, to ensure that they are not bent or badly worn. The pegs which engage with the cam channels are integral with the forks therefore if they are worn the forks must be renewed. Under normal conditions, the gear selector mechanism is unlikely to wear quickly.

9   The tracks in the selector drum, with which the selector forks engage, should not show any undue signs of wear unless neglect has led to under-lubrication of the gearbox. Check the tension of the gearchange pawl, gearchange arm and drum stopper arm springs. Weakness in the springs will lead to imprecise gear selection. Check the condition of the gear stopper arm roller and on the pins in the change drum end with which it engages. It is unlikely that wear will take place here except after considerable mileage.

10 Check the condition of the kickstart components. If slipping has been encountered, a worn ratchet and pawl will invariably be traced as the cause. Any other damage or wear to the components will be self-evident. If either the ratchet or pawl is found to be faulty, both components must be replaced as a pair. Examine the kickstart return spring, which should be renewed if there is any doubt about its condition.

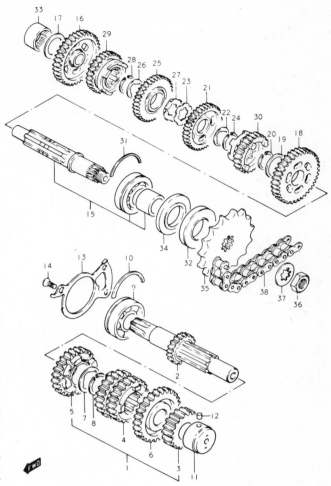

Fig. 1.10 Gearbox assembly – component parts

1 Mainshaft	19 Washer
2 Mainshaft 1st gear pinion (13T)	20 Circlip
3 Mainshaft 2nd gear pinion (18T)	21 Layshaft 3rd gear pinion (29T)
4 Mainshaft 4th and 3rd gear pinion (24/21T)	22 Splined washer
5 Mainshaft 5th gear pinion (26T)	23 Locking washer
6 Mainshaft 6th gear pinion (27T)	24 Circlip
7 Splined washer	25 Layshaft 4th gear pinion (27T)
8 Circlip	26 Splined washer
9 Bearing	27 Locking washer
10 Bearing half-clip	28 Circlip
11 Needle roller bearing	29 Layshaft 5th gear pinion (25T)
12 Dowel pin	30 Layshaft 6th gear pinion (23T)
13 Bearing retainer plate	31 Bearing half-clip
14 Countersunk screw – 3off	32 Oil seal
15 Layshaft	33 Needle roller bearing
16 Layshaft 1st gear pinion (32T)	34 Oil seal
17 Thrust washer	35 Gearbox sprocket (16T)
18 Layshaft 2nd gear pinion (32T)	36 Nut
	37 Lockwasher
	38 Final drive chain

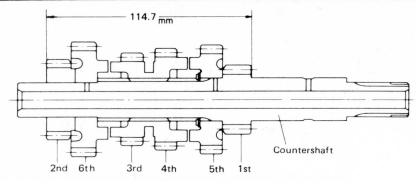

Fig. 1.11 Adjustment of mainshaft gearcluster length

30 Examination and renovation: clutch assembly

1 After an extended period of use the clutch linings will wear and promote clutch slip. The clutch plates should be measured with a vernier gauge or pair of calipers to ascertain the extent of wear. The measurement of the thickness for the inserted (friction) plates and the maximum wear limits are as follows:

Inserted plate width 2.9 - 3.1 mm (0.114 - 0.122 in)
Wear limit 2.7 mm (0.106 in)

If the plate width is less than the specified minimum, then the plate must be renewed.

2 The plain clutch plates should not show any evidence of overheating (blueing). If they do, check them for overall flatness by placing each plate on a flat surface. In the event of the plates being warped by more than 0.3 mm (0.012 in) they should be renewed.

3 Check the free length of each clutch spring. If the springs have shortened to a length less than the specified minimum, they must be renewed, preferably as a set.

Clutch spring Free length   38.4 mm (1.51 in)
Wear limit   37.0 mm (1.46 in)

4 Check the condition of the clutch centre spacer and the external caged needle roller bearing. If wear is evident in these components, they should be renewed. The bearing and spacer upon which the oil pump drive gear (fitted behind the clutch) is mounted should be checked similarly.

5 Check the condition of the slots in the outer surface of the clutch centre and the inner surfaces of the outer drum. In an extreme case, clutch chatter may have caused the tongues of the inserted plates to make indentations in the slots of the outer drum, or the tongues of the plain plates to indent the slots of the clutch centre. These indentations will trap the clutch plates as they are freed and impair clutch action. If the damage is only slight the indentations can be removed by careful work with a file and the burrs removed from the tongues of the clutch plates in similar fashion. More extensive damage will necessitate renewal of the parts concerned.

6 Check the clutch release thrust bearing in the pressure plate. If play is evident or the bearing rotates roughly, it should be renewed.

7 The clutch release mechanism in the clutch cover does not normally require attention, provided that it is greased from time to time. If the unit fails, it should be renewed as a complete assembly.

31 Examination and renovation: primary drive gears

1 Inspect the primary drive pinion and the pinion affixed to the clutch outer drum, for worn or chipped teeth. It is probable that if damage or wear is found in one pinion, similar problems will occur on the other.

2 Check the driven pinion shock-absorber springs for breakage or excessive slack. If movement can be felt between the pinion and the clutch outer drum, renewal is required.

3 The primary driven pinion, shock-absorber and the clutch outer drum are supplied as a complete unit. If one component is damaged the whole unit must be renewed.

32 Examination and renovation: crankcase covers

1 The right-hand and left-hand crankcase covers and the inspection covers are unlikely to become damaged unless the machine is dropped or involved in an accident. Cracks in a casing can be repaired easily by special aluminium welding, providing the damage is not too extensive and care is taken to prevent distortion.

2 The covers are lightly polished and lacquered before leaving the factory. Badly scratched covers can be refurbished using a single cut file treated with chalk to prevent clogging, and finished off with fine emery paper and metal polish or aluminium cleaner. If required, the cases can be relacquered, using an aerosol paint spray.

33 Engine reassembly: general

1 Before reassembly of the engine/gear unit is commenced, the various component parts should be cleaned thoroughly and placed on a sheet of clean paper, close to the working area.

2 Make sure all traces of old gaskets have been removed and that the mating surfaces are clean and undamaged. One of the best ways to remove old gasket cement is to apply a rag soaked in methylated spirit. This acts as a solvent and will ensure that the cement is removed without resort to scraping and the consequent risk of damage.

If a gasket becomes bonded to the surface through the effects of heat and age, a new sharp scalpel blade should be used to effect removal. Old gasket compound can also be removed using a soft brass wire brush of the type used for cleaning suede shoes. A considerable amount of scrubbing can take place without fear of damaging the mating surfaces.

3 Gather together all the necessary tools and have available an oil can filled with clean engine oil. Make sure that all new gaskets and oil seals are to hand, also all replacement parts required. Nothing is more frustrating than having to stop in the middle of a reassembly sequence because a vital gasket or replacement has been overlooked.

4 Make sure that the reassembly area is clean and that there is adequate working space. Refer to the torque and clearance settings wherever they are given. Many of the smaller bolts are easily sheared if overtightened. Always use the correct size screwdriver or bit for the crosshead screws never an ordinary screwdriver or punch. If the existing screws show evidence of maltreatment in the past, it is advisable to renew them as a complete set.

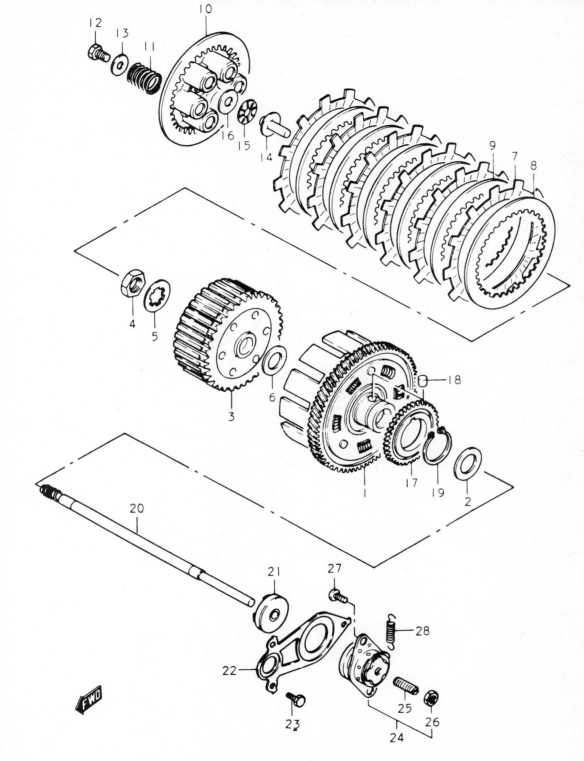

Fig. 1.12 Clutch assembly – component parts

1 Primary driven pinion	8 Plain backing plate	15 Thrust bearing	22 Oil seal retainer plate
2 Thrust washer	9 Plain plate – 5 off	16 Thrust washer	23 Screw – 3 off
3 Clutch centre	10 Pressure plate	17 Oil pump drive pinion	24 Lifting mechanism
4 Nut	11 Spring – 6 off	18 Drive pin	25 Adjusting screw
5 Lockwasher	12 Bolt – 6 off	19 Circlip	26 Locknut
6 Thrust washer	13 Washer – 6 off	20 Pushrod	27 Screw – 2 off
7 Friction plate – 6 off	14 Thrust piece	21 Oil seal	28 Spring

34 Engine reassembly: replacing the gear change drum and internal selector components and chain tensioner blade

1   Lubricate the gearchange drum needle roller bearing and then insert the change drum into the casing from the primary drive side of the upper casing. If, on examination, the change pins were found to be worn and the pins and retainer plate have been removed, do not refit them at this stage. The pins should be fitted in a special sequence, as described in Section 41 of this Chapter.

2   Insert the selector fork rod, locating it with each of the three selector forks as it is pushed home. The shortest of the forks is fitted in the centre of the rod, flanked on either side by the two long forks. Of the two longer forks, the one with the two strengthening webs is fitted to the right (primary drive side) of the centre fork. The guide pin on each fork must be pointing rearwards and engaged with the appropriate channel in the change drum.

3   After replacing the selector rod, fit and tighten the rod securing screw which is located in the primary drive chamber wall. Apply a locking fluid to the screw threads before installing. Invert the crankcase half and fit the change drum neutral detent plunger, spring and housing bolt. Do not omit the sealing washer fitted to the bolt. Rotate the change drum so that it is in the neutral position.

4   Install the chain tensioner blade, securing it by means of the single nut.

35 Engine reassembly: replacing the gear shaft assemblies

1   Position the upper crankcase half so that it rests on the cylinder holding down studs and the rear of the casing. Before refitting, the gearshafts must be assembled as completed sub-assemblies, including the gear pinions, bearings and oil seals. The oil seal lips should be lubricated before being installed, to prevent damage. Note that the layshaft is fitted with two oil seals placed side by side. The inner seal which abuts against the drive side bearing must be positioned with the castellated projections facing outwards. The outer seal should be placed with the concave side facing inwards.

2   Install the bearing securing half clips in the casing grooves and lower the gear shafts into place, either individually or as a meshed pair. Three of the four bearings are fitted with a single location pin each. Arrange each bearing so that the pin rests in the notch provided in the casing wall. The mainshaft needle roller bearing is located by a peg which is a push fit in the outer race and in the bearing housing.

3   Do not omit the clutch pushrod oil seal which is located at the left-hand end of the mainshaft.

34.1 Lubricate and insert the gearchange drum

34.2 Position selector forks and install selector rod

34.3a Secure rod by means of special screw

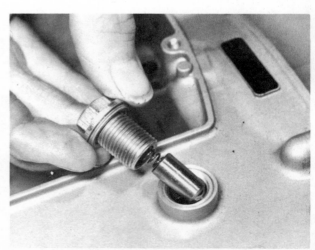

34.3b Replace detent unit after placing drum in neutral position

34.4a Install the chain tensioner blade ...

34.4b ... securing it with single nut

35.2a Install mainshaft right-hand and ...

35.2b ...layshaft left-hand bearing half-clips

35.2c Layshaft oil seals must be fitted as shown

35.2d Replace the completed layshaft

35.2e Position needle roller bearing pin and ...

35.2f ...ball bearing pin in housing recesses

35.2g Fit mainshaft as a completed unit and ...

35.3 ... replace the pushrod oil seal

36 Engine reassembly: replacing the crankshaft and balance shaft

1   Lubricate the main bearings thoroughly and also the crank-shaft end onto which the oil seal is to be fitted. The seal should be placed with the garter spring facing inwards.
2   Insert the three main bearing locating pegs into the holes provided in the casing. The right-hand main bearing is located by a half clip in a manner similar to that of the gearbox ball bearings. In addition, a locating pin is fitted which must be positioned in the recess adjacent to the bearing housing.
3   Fit the cam drive chain over the crankshaft so that it meshes with the drive sprocket. Grasp the crankshaft at both ends and lower the completed assembly into position. Ensure that the main bearing outer races engage correctly with the locating dowels. A tiny punch mark is provided on each main bearing outer race, diametrically opposed to the centre of the dowel hole. Lining up all three marks in a perfectly straight line will aid correct location of the bearings. It should be noted however that on the machine featured in this manual, one punch mark had been made inaccurately. Even when the crank-shaft was correctly positioned the dots did not align. This should, of course, only be attempted after ensuring correct loca-tion of the pegs and the half clip.

4   Fit the balance shaft left-hand bearing half clip into the groove in the crankcase upper half. Both bearings are located by pins similar to that used on the crankshaft journal ball bearing. Lower the complete balance shaft into place so that the pinion engages with the drive pinion on the crankshaft. To ensure that engine balance is correct, the relative positions of the balance shaft and crankshaft must be timed together. To facilitate this a punch mark is provided on the face of each pinion. Ensure that these marks align exactly when the balance shaft is finally in position.

37 Engine reassembly: replacing the kickstart assembly, oil pick-up and baffle plates

1   The components listed in the heading must all be fitted into the crankcase lower half before the crankcase halves can be joined.
2   If the kickstart shaft was dismantled for inspection, it must be reassembled before fitting into the crankcase. Refit the com-ponents into the kickstart shaft in the order shown in the accompanying illustration. Note that the ratchet pawl has a punch mark on the outer face which must be aligned with a similar mark on the shaft splines. After assembly, the kickstart

shaft unit must be inserted through the gearbox wall in the crankcase lower casing. Once the kickstart shaft is in place, fit the pawl plate and the two countersunk screws. The screw threads must be treated with a locking fluid before insertion. Install the shaft flange bush and insert and tighten the three countersunk screws. These too should be treated with locking fluid. Three similar screws are used to retain the bearing retainer plate within the same casing. These screws are longer. Take care not to fit the incorrect screws. Replace the circlip in the shaft groove adjacent to the shaft flanged bush.

3   Replace the gauze screen on the oil pick-up funnel, securing it by means of the tag and two screws. Check that the sealing O-ring is in place in the upper end of the funnel and fit the unit into place.

4   Refitting the baffle plates is a straightforward operation. The screw threads should be treated with locking fluid to ensure total security.

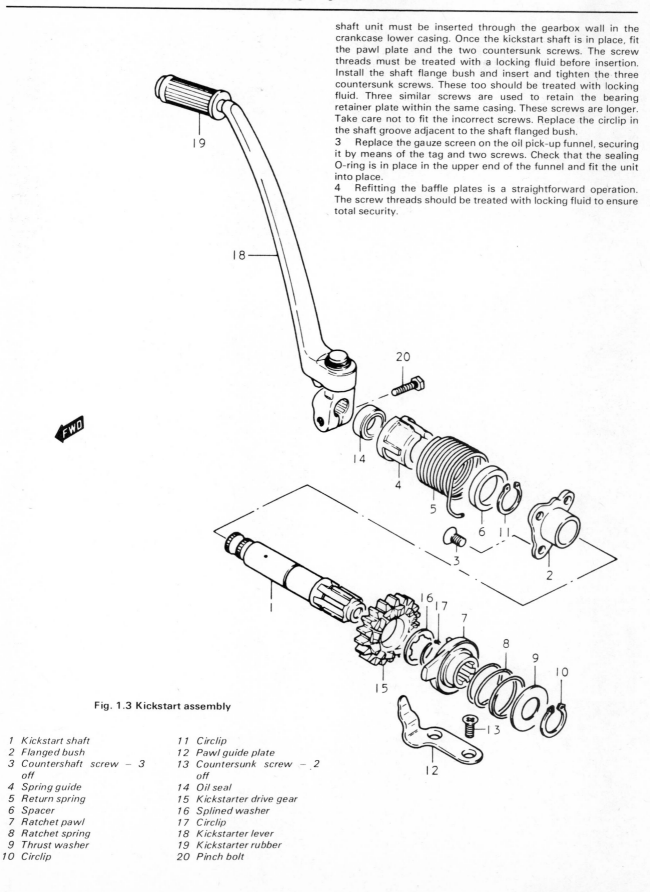

Fig. 1.3 Kickstart assembly

1 Kickstart shaft
2 Flanged bush
3 Countershaft screw – 3 off
4 Spring guide
5 Return spring
6 Spacer
7 Ratchet pawl
8 Ratchet spring
9 Thrust washer
10 Circlip
11 Circlip
12 Pawl guide plate
13 Countersunk screw – 2 off
14 Oil seal
15 Kickstarter drive gear
16 Splined washer
17 Circlip
18 Kickstarter lever
19 Kickstarter rubber
20 Pinch bolt

36.2a Install main bearing location pins and ...

36.2b ... right-hand bearing locating half-clip

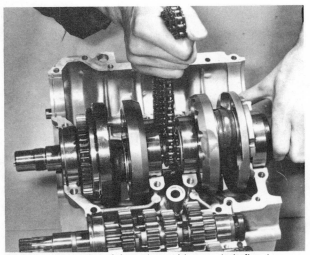

36.3a Lower crankshaft into place with cam chain fitted

36.3b Note alignment dot on each bearing outer race

36.4a Replace balance shaft bearing half clip and ...

36.4b ... lower shaft into position so that ...

36.4c ... the timing marks are in exact alignment

36.4d Bearing pins must be positioned as shown

37.2a Ensure kickstart pawl aligns with shaft when reassembling

37.2b Secure kickstart components with circlip

37.2c Insert kickstart shaft into casing and fit bush

37.2d Retain shaft by means of circlip and fit screws

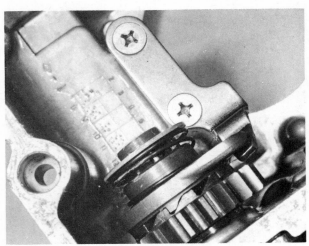

37.2e Replace pawl guide plate, held by two screws

37.3 Install oil pick-up funnel; do not omit 'O' ring

38 Engine reassembly: joining the crankcase halves

1   Carefully clean the crankcase halves mating surfaces. Replace the two hollow locating dowels, tapping them into position carefully so as not to distort them. If the dowels have become slightly burred they should be cleaned up with a small file.

2   Smear the upper crankcase half mating face with a thin layer of jointing compound. Suzuki recommend that Suzuki Bond No. 4 be used to make a joint. A good quality non-hardening compound will make a suitable substitute. Fit a new small O-ring into the recess to the front of the mainshaft assembly. Let the gasket compound set for at least 10 mins and then lower the upper casing into place. Use a rawhide mallet or the flat of the hand to tap the casing fully home. Check that all the shafts are able to rotate freely. Fit the crankcase retaining bolts to the lower crankcase. Tighten the 8 mm bolts evenly a little at a time, following the numerical sequence stamped on the casing adjacent to each bolt, commencing with No. 1. Tighten the remaining bolts and then invert the crankcase and fit the upper bolts. All crankcase bolts should be tightened to the torque settings specified.

Crankcase bolts

8 mm	2.0 kg m (14.5 ft lbs)
6 mm	1.0 kg m (7.2 ft lbs)

Do not omit the single nut fitted to the left-hand wall of the gearbox.

39 Engine reassembly: replacing the oil strainer screen, cover and oil filter

1   If the oil strainer screen was not fitted to the pick-up funnel before funnel replacement, it may now be installed. Place the screen in position and twist it to the right a few degrees so that the locating tab engages correctly. Fit and tighten the two retaining screws.

2   Place a new gasket on the screen access cover and secure it by means of the three bolts.

3   Install a new oil filter in the chamber within the lower crankcase half. Check that the chamber cover is in good condition and fit the filter location spring and the cover. The cover is secured by three dome nuts. If the drain plug was removed it should now be refitted.

4   The engine should now be inverted so that it is resting in the normal position on the workbench, supported as required by wooden blocks.

40 Engine reassembly: replacing the oil pump and kickstart return spring

1   The oil pump must be re-installed in the primary drive casing as a complete unit, either before or after the driven gear is fitted. The driven gear is retained by a circlip on the shaft end, and is located by a drive pin which passes through the shaft, engaging with a recess in the rear face of the pinion.

2   Place a new O-ring in each of the casing recesses against the wall to which the pump is secured. Omission of the O-rings will lead to lubrication failure. Position the oil pump and fit and tighten the three mounting screws. It is recommended that locking fluid be used on the mounting screws.

3   Slide the kickstart spring over the shaft, with the inner turned end towards the outside. Rotate the kickstart shaft as far as possible in a clockwise direction and then insert the inner turned end of the spring into the innermost cross-drilled hole in the shaft. Grasp the outer turned end of the spring with a stout pair of pliers and tension the spring in a clockwise direction until the spring end can be inserted into the anchor hole in the casing.

4   Slide the spring guide into position, ensuring that it is fully home. The guide outer edge should be approximately in line with the outer coil of the spring.

38.2a 'O' ring **must** be fitted before ...

38.2b ... lowering crankcase half into position

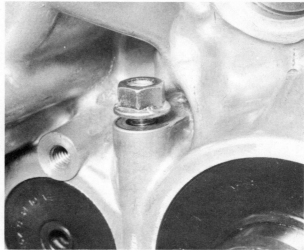

38.2c Do not forget to fit single crankcase nut

40.2a Place two new 'O' rings into the casing before ...

40.2b ... replacing the oil pump

40.3a Tension kickstart spring and anchor the outer end

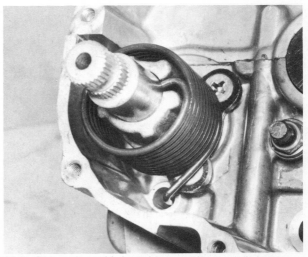

40.3b Slide spring guide into place ensuring it is fully home

41 Engine reassembly: replacing the gear selector external components

1   Refit the mainshaft bearing retainer plate into the primary drive chamber, using locking fluid on the three countersunk screws.

2   Position the change drum guide plate in the casing and insert and screw in lightly the rearmost retaining bolt. Grease the splined end of the gearchange arm so that when it passes through the oil seal in the left-hand wall of the gearbox, the sealing lip will not be damaged. Insert the gearchange shaft, complete with the pawl arm and return spring, into the primary drive chamber. The change arm centraliser spring must be fitted on the arm as shown. When in position the spring arms must lie either side of the anchor peg in the casing. Push the assembly fully home, simultaneously pulling back the pawl arm so that it clears the end of the change drum and engages with the change pins. If the change pins and retaining plate were removed for pin renewal, the replacement pins can now be fitted, using the correct positioning procedure.

3   Install the change drum stopper arm. The pivot bolt is of the shouldered type and serves also as the change drum guide plate front securing bolt. Tighten both bolts and check that the stopper arm is free to move and has not been trapped by the bolt shoulder. Reconnect the arm return spring with the anchor lug on the bearing retainer plate. Of the six change pins, one is of differing dimensions, having a relieved portion at one end. It is against this recess that the stopper arm roller abuts when the gearbox is in neutral. Check that the gearbox is still in the neutral position and then insert the neutral pin in the change drum pin hole nearest to the stopper arm roller. Push the roller hard up against the recess so that the two components self-align. Insert the five remaining pins in the holes provided. Position the pin retainer plate on the end of the change drum so that the punched depression engages with the neutral pin. Fit and tighten the central screw.

42 Engine reassembly: replacing the primary drive pinion and clutch

1   Fit the Woodruff key into the keyway in the crankshaft right-hand mainshaft. Slide the pinion into place so that the key on the shaft engages with the keyway in the pinion. The pinion should be fitted with the greater diameter face outwards. Replace the special washer, concave side against the pinion, and fit and tighten the nut. Lock the crankshaft by means of a close fitting bar through one small end eye.

2   Fit the heavy washer onto the clutch shaft (mainshaft). If the oil pump drive pinion was removed it must be refitted to the rear of the clutch outer drum before continuing. Insert the pinion drive pin and fit the pinion so that the raised boss is towards the clutch. Secure the pinion by means of the circlip. Position the clutch outer drum on the clutch shaft so that it meshes with the primary drive pinion. Likewise, the oil pump drive pinion must be meshed with the driven gear.

3   Install a heavy thrust washer on the clutch shaft and then refit the clutch centre boss onto the clutch shaft splines. Fit the tab washer and then fit and tighten the centre nut. Use the same procedure for tightening the nut as was used for loosening. Place the machine in top gear and temporarily refit the final drive sprocket onto the output shaft. After tightening the nut, do not omit to bend up the tab washer to secure the nut in place. Before replacing the clutch plates note that one plain plate is 2.0 mm thick whereas the remaining plain plates are 1.5 mm thick. The heavier plate - the only one not marked with a small circle on one face - must be fitted first, at the back of the clutch drum. Replace the remaining clutch plates one at a time, commencing with a friction (inserted) plate followed by a plain plate and so on, alternately. Grease the clutch operating pushrod and insert it into the hollow clutch shaft. The scrolled end can be

placed only on the right-hand side of the engine. Lubricate the clutch thrust piece and fit it, together with the thrust bearing and shim. Refit the clutch pressure plate, and the clutch springs, washers and bolts. Tighten the bolts fully.

4   The primary drive cover can now be replaced. Lubricate the contact breaker and kickstart oil seals and the primary drive gears with engine oil and then fit a new gasket to the mating surface. Push the cover into position on the two hollow locating dowels and then fit the screws. The screws should be tightened evenly, in a diagonal sequence, to help prevent distortion. Do not omit the single screw located in the contact breaker housing.

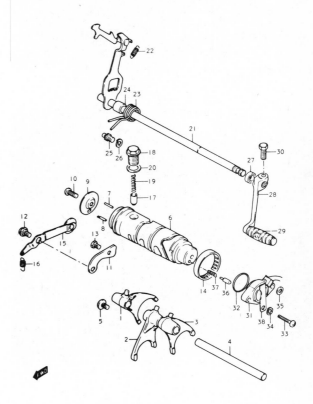

Fig. 1.14 Gearchange mechanism – component parts

1 Selector fork	21 Gearchange shaft/change arm
2 Selector fork	
3 Selector fork	22 Spring
4 Selector fork rod	23 Centralising spring
5 Screw	24 Collar
6 Gearchange drum	25 Spring anchor
7 Change pin – 5 off	26 Spring washer
8 Stepped change pin	27 Oil seal
9 Pin plate	28 Gearlever
10 Screw	29 Boot
11 Guide plate	30 Pinch bolt
12 Shouldered bolt	31 Gear position and neutral indicator switch
13 Screw	
14 Caged needle roller bearing	32 'O' ring
	33 Screw – 2 off
15 Drum detent arm	34 Spring washer – 2 off
16 Spring	35 Washer
17 Detent plunger	36 Switch contact
18 Detent holder	37 Spring
19 Spring	38 Lead clamp
20 Sealing washer	

41.1 Replace the bearing retainer plate

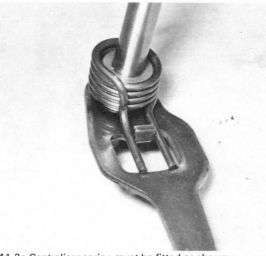
41.2a Centraliser spring must be fitted as shown

41.2b Fit change pawl arm and drum guide plate

41.3a Fit stopper arm so roller abuts against shouldered pin

41.3b Note how pin plate locates with special pin

41.3c Gear selector mechanism; general view

42.1a Insert Woodruff key into crankshaft and ...

42.1b ... slide pinion into place

42.1c Fit washer with convex side outermost

42.2a Oil pump pinion is located by drive pin and secured by a circlip

42.2b Fit clutch backing washer followed by ...

42.2c ...clutch outer drum and thrust washer

42.3a Replace centre and fit lockwasher and nut

42.3b Grease and insert clutch pushrod and ...

42.3c ... the thrust washer and bearing

42.3d Insert clutch plates commencing with heavy backing plate

42.3e Fit plain and friction plates alternately

42.3f Replace clutch pressure plate and then ...

42.3g ... fit and tighten springs, bolts and washer

42.4a Install new gasket before fitting primary drive cover

42.4b Do not omit to tighten hidden screw

43 Engine reassembly: replacing the ATU and contact breaker assembly

1   Position the ATU against the end of the crankshaft so that the drive pin projecting from the shaft end engages with the recess in the rear of the unit. Hold the ATU in position and replace the centre bolt and the hexagonal engine turning piece. To tighten the bolt, pass a close fitting bar through one small-end eye, bearing down on two wooden blocks placed across the crankcase mouth. This will lock the crankshaft.
2   Position the contact breaker stator plate (the base plate) close to the engine and feed the low tension leads through the hole in the rear of the contact breaker housing. The stator plate should be positioned so that the contact breaker pivots are above the cam
3   If, on dismantling, a punch mark was made on the stator plate aligning with a similar mark on the casing, these marks should be realigned and the two retaining screws fitted. It is probable that the ignition timing will be correct but a check must be made as a precautionary measure. Where no alignment marks were made, ignition timing should be set as a matter of course, as described in Chapter 3, Section 7. Note that the lower timing adjustment screw serves to secure the low tension

lead guide clamp. Do not fit the contact breaker cover before fitting and timing the valves.

44 Engine reassembly: replacing the starter motor, starter motor clutch and intermediate gear and alternator

1   Place the starter clutch pinion bearing thrust washer onto the left-hand end of the crankshaft so that the face with the chamfered inner radius is towards the main bearing. Lubricate the double needle roller bearings and fit them, together with the clutch pinion.
2   Before fitting the combined alternator rotor/starter clutch unit, clean thoroughly the external taper on the crankshaft end and the internal taper in the alternator rotor. Position the rotor/clutch assembly on the shaft, turning it anti-clockwise so that the three clutch rollers slide easily onto the pinion boss. Insert and tighten the rotor centre bolt. The correct torque wrench setting is 6.0 - 7.0 kg m (43.0 – 50.6 lb ft).
3   Grease the starter motor boss O-ring and insert the starter motor into the casing. Take care not to trap the contact breaker lead. Push the motor fully home and then fit and tighten the two securing bolts. The bolts should be treated with a sealing compound to prevent oil seepage from the gearbox, into which they protrude. Route the starter cable and low tension leads through the relieved casing edge and then fit the starter motor cover.
4   Place the intermediate double gear on its stub shaft and fit one thrust washer either side of the gear. Position the assembly in the casing with the finer toothed gear to the rear of the starter clutch pinion, and push the stub shaft fully home into the casing recess.
5   Fit a new gasket to the crankcase after checking that the single hollow locating dowel has been inserted towards the rear of the casing. Replace the cover and fit and tighten the screws.

45 Engine reassembly: replacing the gear indicator switch

1   Before refitting the switch, replace the oil seal retainer plate which is fitted to the outside of the gearbox left-hand wall. After tightening the bolts bend up the ears of the plate to secure them.
2   Position the O-ring in the switch recess and insert the contact and contact spring in the hole in the change drum end. Replace the neutral indicator body and tighten down the two retaining screws. Note that the switch body left-hand screw retains also a short flat clamp, provided to guide the alternator leads. Before tightening the screw, route the leads over the top of the switch, securing them with the clamp plate.

43.1 Position ATU engaged with drive pin in crankshaft end

44.1a Refit copper washer and the two bearings

44.1b The copper washer must be fitted with chamfered side innermost

44.1c Lubricate bearings and slide spur gear into position

44.2a Turn rotor anti-clockwise to facilitate refitting

44.2b Fit alternator rotor centre bolt and washer

44.3 Install and secure the starter motor

44.4 Replace starter motor idler gear with washer both sides

45.1 Fit oil seal plate and secure bolts by bending up tags

45.2a Do not omit contact and spring or 'O' ring on gear indicator switch

45.2b Secure wiring leads above switch by means of plate clamp

46 Engine reassembly: replacing the pistons and the cylinder block

1   Fit the piston rings to each piston, commencing with the three-piece oil control ring. The first of the three parts to be fitted should be the corrugated spacer band. Where the N type spacer is used, ensure that the band ends are not allowed to overlap when the spacer is in place in the ring groove. Fit the oil control ring side rails one at a time. When fitting the two compression rings, ensure that both are fitted with the R or N mark facing upwards. The two letter marks indicate the manufacturer of the ring. Do not mix rings of different makes in the same engine. The two compression rings are of differing type and cross-section. The upper ring has a chrome plated face which is slightly curved. The 2nd ring is not chrome plated and has a tapered face. Before replacing the pistons, pad the mouths of the crankcase with rag in order to prevent any displaced component from accidentally dropping into the crankcase.

2   Fit the pistons in their original order with the arrow on the piston crown pointing toward the front of the engine.

3   If the gudgeon pins are a tight fit, first warm the pistons to expand the metal. Oil the gudgeon pins and small end bearing surfaces, also the piston bosses, before fitting the pistons.

4   Always use new circlips **never** the originals. Always check that the circlips are located properly in their grooves in the piston boss. A displaced circlip will cause severe damage to the cylinder bore, and possibly an engine seizure.

5   Install the two sealing rings in the recesses surrounding the outer rear cylinder studs and then fit a new cylinder base gasket over the studs. Check that the two hollow locating dowels are fitted to the outer front holding down studs. A new O ring should be placed on each of the two cylinder bore spigots. Push the O rings fully home, so that they seat correctly in the grooves provided.

6   Arrange the piston ring gaps as shown in the accompaning diagram, in order to maintain the best sealing characteristics. Using clean engine oil, lubricate thoroughly the cylinder bores. Lift the cylinder block up onto the studs and support it there whilst the camshaft chain is threaded through the tunnel between the bores. This task is best achieved by using a piece of stiff wire to hook the chain through, and pull up through the tunnel. The chain must engage with the crankshaft drive sprocket.

7   The cylinder bores have a generous lead in for the pistons at the bottom, and although it is an advantage on an engine such as this to use the special Suzuki ring compressor, in the absence of this it is possible to gently lead the pistons into the bores working across from one side. Great care has to be taken NOT to put too much pressure on the fitted piston rings. When the pistons have finally engaged, remove the rag padding from the crankcase mouths and lower the cylinder block still further until it seats firmly on the base gasket.

8   Take care to anchor the camshaft chain throughout this operation to save the chain dropping down into the crankcase.

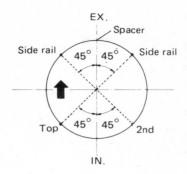

Fig. 1.16 Positioning of piston ring end gaps

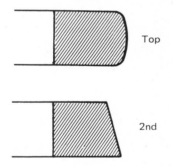

Fig. 1.15 Piston ring profile

46.2 Arrow on piston crown must face forwards

46.4a Pad crankcase mouth before inserting gudgeon pin

46.4b Ensure circlip is correctly located in the groove; this isn't

46.5a Place new 'O' ring on each cylinder bore spigot

46.56 Fit new gasket and seals and then lower block into position

47 Engine reassembly: replacing the cylinder head

1   Place a new cylinder head gasket in position on the holding down studs. The gasket is marked TOP and should be fitted accordingly. Replace the cam tunnel rectangular seal.

2   Slide the cylinder head down the studs into position whilst guiding the cam chain through the tunnel. Secure the chain once again. Fit the cylinder head holding nuts, washers and bolts. It should be noted that the four outer studs are fitted with copper washers, to prevent oil seepage from the stud holes which serve also as oilways.

   Tighten the cylinder head nuts evenly, in the sequence shown in the accompanying illustration, to a setting of 3.5 - 4.0 kg m (25.3 - 29.0 lb ft). Finally, tighten the two 6 mm bolts to 0.7 - 1.1 kg m (5.0 - 8.0 lb ft).

3   Insert the cam chain tensioner forward blade into the cylinder head central tunnel so that the lower end engages in the recess in the guide seat and the upper end locates with the recesses each side of the tunnel. Make a special check that the lower end of the blade is restrained; if it is allowed to float in operation the cam chain may become damaged.

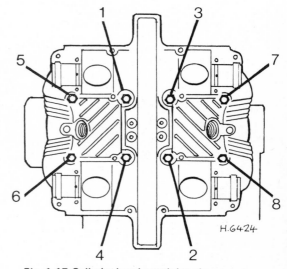

Fig. 1.17 Cylinder head nut tightening sequence

47.1 Install a new head gasket and cam chain tunnel seal

47.2a Lower the cylinder head into position

47.2b Note copper washers under domed cylinder head nuts

47.3 Ensure cam chain guide blade locates correctly at top and bottom

48 Engine reassembly: replacing the camshafts and timing the valves

1   Lubricate thoroughly and insert the cam followers into their original guide tunnels in the cylinder head. Provided the followers are fitted squarely, very little pressure should be required to insert them in the tunnels. Do not attempt to tap (even lightly) a follower into place as it will probably jam solidly. Removal is then very difficult. Fit also the original adjuster shims.

2   Because the cam chain is endless, the camshaft replacement and valve timing operations must be made simultaneously. Fit a spanner to the engine turning hexagon and rotate the engine forwards until the T mark on the R side of the ATU is in **exact** alignment with the index mark on the static plate. In this position No. 1 cylinder (RH cylinder) is at TDC. Whilst turning the engine, the cam chain will have to be hand fed so that it does not become snagged or bunched up.

3   Select the exhaust camshaft (marked EX) and feed it through the cam chain. Pull the forward run of the chain taut and mesh the cam sprocket to the chain so that when the camshaft is lying across the bearing housings, the 2 marked arrow is pointing vertically. Insert the inlet camshaft through the cam chain in a similar way. To mesh the sprocket in the correct

place, count the chain roller pins from the exhaust camshaft to the inlet camshaft start with the pin directly above the 2 marked arrow on the exhaust camshaft sprocket and count to the 20th pin along the chain. Mesh the 3 marked arrow on the inlet sprocket with the 20th pin. Provided that the crankshaft has not moved during this procedure, the valve timing is now correct.

4   The two bearing caps holding each camshaft can now be refitted. Note that each cap is marked A, B, C or D and each should be fitted to the bearing housing similarly marked. The caps should be placed so that the letters are not inverted relative to one another. Great care should be taken when tightening down the bearing cap bolts. If, due to the position of a camshaft, a camlobe is in contact with its cam follower and preventing correct seating of the shaft, the bolts should be tightened evenly and diagonally, a little at a time, allowing neither the caps nor the camshaft to tilt. The bolts should be tightened to a final torque of 0.8 - 1.2 kg m (5.6 - 6.8 lb ft). After tightening the cap bolts, re-check the valve timing.

5   Fit the cam chain tensioner jockey sprocket ensuring that the sprocket is fitted in its original position and tighten the holding bolts to 0.6 - 0.8 kg m (4.3 - 5.8 lb ft). The performance of the rubber damper blocks upon which is mounted the sprocket depends upon the bolts being tightened to the correct torque.

48.1 Fit adjuster pads with etched number downwards

48.3 Install both camshafts, timing them simultaneously

48.4 Bearing caps are marked and should be fitted accordingly

48.5 Tighten sprocket mounting bolts to specified torque

Fig. 1.18 Valve timing procedure

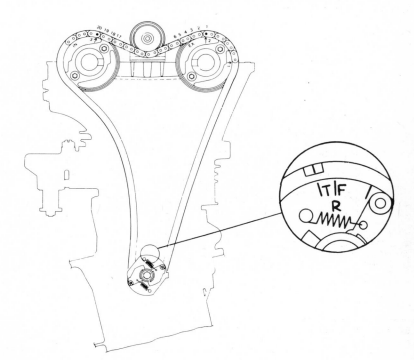

49 Engine reassembly: replacing and adjusting the cam chain tensioner

1   Hold the cam chain tensioner in one hand and whilst restraining the plunger rod, slacken the locking screw a few turns. Push the plunger inwards fully, simultaneously rotating the knurled adjuster wheel anti-clockwise. Continue turning until the plunger is fully retracted and the knurled adjuster has moved as far as possible. Tighten the lock screw to secure the pushrod.

2   Fit a new gasket to the tensioner body flange and install the completed unit to the rear of the cylinder block. Tighten the securing bolts evenly, to a torque setting of 1.0 kg m (7.2 lb ft).

3   With the tensioner fitted to the engine, unscrew the locking screw $\frac{1}{4} - \frac{1}{2}$ a turn so that the plunger is free to move forwards under tension from the spring. Without allowing further rotation of the locking screw, tighten the locknut.

4   The cam chain tensioner is now set for automatic adjustment in service. To check whether the unit is functioning correctly, rotate the engine backwards to take up all the slack in the rear run of the chain. Whilst turning the engine backwards, rotate the knurled adjuster wheel slowly in an anti-clockwise direction as far as possible. Now turn the engine in a forward direction, which will have the effect of slackening the chain on the rear run. The knurled adjuster wheel should be seen to rotate in a clockwise direction as the plunger moves out and automatically tensions the chain.

5   **WARNING.** After initial adjustment of the cam chain tensioner, the tensioner will continue to function automatically. **DO NOT** under any circumstances rotate the knurled adjuster wheel either clockwise or anticlockwise except when making this adjustment in the prescribed manner. Rotation of the wheel except at this stage will cause excessive chain tightness and will lead to tensioner and chain damage.

49.1 Install tensioner with plunger held fully compressed by screw

49.3 Slacken off screw $\frac{1}{4} - \frac{1}{2}$ turn before tightening locknut

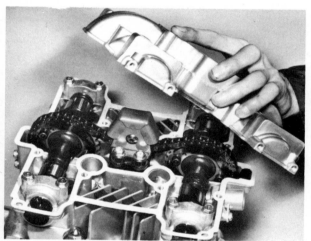
49.5a Refit camshaft cover only after checking valve clearance

49.5b Fit new gasket before refitting the breather cover

50 Engine reassembly: checking and adjusting the valve clearances

1   The clearance between each cam and cam follower must be checked and if necessary adjusted by removal of the existing adjuster pad and replacement by a pad of suitable thickness. Make the clearance check and adjustment of each valve in sequence and then go on to the next valve. As shown in the diagram in the Routine Maintenance section both operations should be carried out with the cam lobe in question placed in one of two alternative positions.

2   Using a feeler gauge, verify and record the clearance at the first valve. If the clearance is incorrect, not being within the range 0.03 – 0.08 mm (0.001 – 0.003 in), the adjuster pad must be removed and replaced by a shim of suitable thickness. A special tool is available (Suzuki part no. 09916-64510) which should be pushed between the camshaft adjacent to the cam lobe and the raised edge of the cam follower, to allow removal of the shim. If the special tool is not available, a simple substitute may be fabricated from steel plate. The final form of the tool which has a handle approximately 6 inches long, is shown in the photograph accompanying the cam adjustment section in the Routine Maintenance Chapter. The Suzuki tool should be pushed into position, depressing and securing the cam follower in one operation. Where a home-made tool is used, the cam follower should be depressed by inserting a suitable lever between the adjuster pad and the cam lobe. The tool is then inserted to secure the cam follower whilst the adjuster pad is removed. Before installing either type of tool, rotate the cam follower so that the slot in the follower raised edge is not obscured by the camshaft. Insert a screwdriver through the slot to displace the adjuster pad.

3   Adjustment pads are available in 20 sizes ranging from 2.15 mm to 3.10 mm, in increments of 0.05 mm. Each pad is identified by a three digit number etched on the reverse face. The number (eg. 235) indicates that the pad thickness is 2.35 mm. To select the correct pad subtract 0.03 mm from the measured clearance and add the resultant figure to that of the existing pad. Select the largest available pad whose thickness is slightly smaller than the final figure. Refer to the table accompanying the Routine Maintenance Section for the selection of available pads.

Although the adjustment pads are available as a set, their price is prohibitive. It is recommended that pads are purchased individually, after an accurate assessment of requirements has been made. It is possible that some Suzuki Service Agents will be prepared to exchange used pads for others of the correct size, providing that the original pads are not worn.

4   Before inserting a replacement pad, lubricate both sides thoroughly with engine oil. Always fit the pads with the number downwards, so that it does not become obliterated by the action of the cam. Recheck the valve clearance after fitting the new adjuster pads.

5   After restoring the clearances on each valve refit the camshaft cover. Do not omit the semi-circular seals which are located at each end of the camshaft chambers. Replace the camshaft cover end caps.

---

51 Engine reassembly: replacing the engine in the frame

1   The task of replacing the engine requires three people; two to lift the engine and one to hold the frame steady while the engine is lowered into position.

2   Lift the complete engine unit into the frame from the left-hand side and mount but do not secure the three engine mounting brackets, before inserting the engine bolts. Insert the three long bolts from the left-hand side of the machine and fit the two short central bolts and the special plate bolts. Do not force the bolts into position as this may damage the threads. Use a wooden lever between the frame and the casings, in order to lift the engine and align bolt holes. Tighten the engine mounting bracket bolts first and then the engine bolts. The long spacer is fitted on the left-hand side engine on the upper rear mounting bolt. Do not omit to secure the main earth lead from the battery by means of the upper rear mounting bolt nut.

3   Install the final drive sprocket to the engine with the chain already fitted to it, fit the lockwasher and tighten the locknut. Bend up the lockwasher to secure the nut.

4   Reconnect the starter motor cable with the starter solenoid. Remake the connections from the alternator, contact breaker, neutral indicator and gear indicator switch leads. Ensure that the leads are routed correctly and secured as necessary. Ensure that the colour coding of the wires is followed exactly. Fit the HT leads to the spark plugs.

5   Reconnect the clutch cable with the lifting mechanism in the final drive sprocket cover and then refit the cover. The clutch cable and lifting mechanism should be adjusted as follows: Loosen the locknut on the adjuster screw and rotate the screw inwards until it can be felt to abut against the end of the pushrod. To gain the necessary running clearance unscrew the screw by $\frac{1}{4} - \frac{1}{2}$ a turn and then tighten the locknut. The cable should be adjusted so that there is 4mm ($\frac{1}{16}$ in) play measured between the stock and lever, before the clutch commences lifting. Grease the lifting mechanism by means of the nipple provided before refitting the cover.

6   Before replacing the carburettors, check the air filter box hoses for correct positioning. Each hose is funnel-shaped and should be fitted so that the funnel end within the air filter box curves around inwards in a horizontal plane. When correctly placed, the funnel ends inside the box will face each other. Position the carburettors to the right of the machine and refit the two throttle cables to the wheel type control lever (one cable opens the throttles, and one cable closes them), making sure that the opening cable is fitted to the front, and the closing cable is fitted to the rear of the operating wheel.

Slide the carburettors into place and push them back into the air filter box hoses. Fit the two inlet stubs so that they locate firmly with the carburettors. On late models an O-ring is fitted to the flange face of each stub. Replace the heat sink spacer blocks and the gasket between the block and cylinder head. On early models the heat sink block is made in plastic and a paper gasket is fitted. Later models have an aluminium gasket and an aluminium block. It should be noted that the aluminium block incorporates a small raised portion on the inside bore. This projection, known as a weir, is provided to improve mixture atomization. The block must be fitted so that the weir is at the bottom. Fit and tighten the two socket screws which retain each inlet stub assembly. Tighten the carburettor and air hose screw clamps.

7   Install the connecting hose between the breather cover and the air filter box. Secure the hose by means of the spring clips. The carburettor air vent hoses should be gathered together and retained by a strap to the engine right-hand rear downtube. The two drain pipes should be routed through the gap between the rear of the crankcase and the swinging arm crossmember.

8   Insert a new ring gasket in each exhaust port and then replace the exhaust pipes. Tighten the flange bolts first, followed by the pipe/silencer joint clamp and on 400C models the balance pipe clamps.

9   Replace the kickstart lever and the gear change lever or link arm. Check that both controls are in the correct operating positions before tightening the pinch bolts. Replace the rider's left hand footrest, tightening the securing bolts fully.

10 Lower the petrol tank into place and refit the rear retaining bolt and rubber seat. Connect the petrol pipe and the vacuum tube to the petrol tap unions. Secure the petrol pipe by means of the spring clip.

11 Replace the battery and remake the connections. Give the terminals a coat of petroleum jelly to inhibit corrosion. Fit the frame side cover.

12 Check that the crankcase drain plug has been secured, and then refill the engine with the correct amount of engine oil. The level can be checked through the sight window in the clutch cover which should be between the two marks. Replenish, using the specified quantity of SAE 20W/50 engine oil.

Allow the engine to run for approximately 3 minutes after the initial start-up and then recheck the oil level. Ensure that the

51.2 Remember to fit earth lead to upper rear engine bolt

51.3a Mesh chain with sprocket and fit the sprocket

51.3b Note recess on nut must face inwards

51.5a Reconnect clutch cable with the operating arm

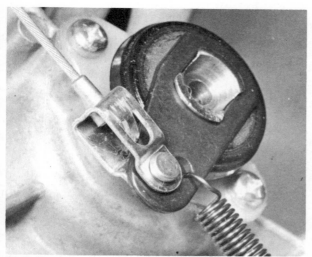
51.5b Bend up tag to secure cable end

51.5c Grease clutch mechanism using the nipple provided before ...

51.5d ... replacing cover, which is held by two screws

51.6a Check that air filter hoses are correctly fitted before ...

51.6b … installing carburettors as a unit

51.6c Ensure that flange 'O' rings (where fitted) are in good condition

51.6d Slide in heat-sink blocks with inlet stub in place

51.6e Opening cable must be fitted at front

machine is standing vertically when checking the level because any angle of lean has a marked effect on the indicated level.

52 Starting and running the rebuilt engine

1   Open the petrol tap, close the carburettor chokes and start the engine, using either the kickstarter or the electric starter. Raise the chokes as soon as the engine will run evenly and keep it running at a low speed for a few minutes to allow oil pressure to build up and the oil to circulate. If the red oil pressure indicator lamp is not extinguished, stop the engine immediately and investigate the lack of oil pressure.
2   The engine may tend to smoke through the exhausts initially, due to the amount of oil used when assembling the various components. The excess of oil should gradually burn away as the engine settles down.
3   Check the exterior of the machine for oil leaks or blowing gaskets. Make sure that each gear engages correctly and that all the controls function effectively, particularly the brakes. This is an essential last check before taking the machine on the road.

53 Taking the rebuilt machine on the road

1   Any rebuilt machine will need time to settle down, even if parts have been replaced in their original order. For this reason it is advisable to treat the machine gently for the first few miles to ensure oil has circulated throughout the lubrication system and that any new parts fitted have begun to bed down.
2   Even greater care is necessary if the engine has been rebored or if a new crankshaft has been fitted. In the case of a rebore, the engine will have to be run-in again, as if the machine were new. This means greater use of the gearbox and a restraining hand on the throttle unit until at least 500 miles have been covered. There is no point in keeping to any set speed limit; the main requirement is to keep a light loading on the engine and to gradually work up performance until the 500 mile mark is reached. These recommendations can be lessened to an extent when only a new crankshaft is fitted. Experience is the best guide since it is easy to tell when an engine is running freely.
3   If at any time a lubrication failure is suspected, stop the engine immediately, and investigate the cause. If an engine is run without oil, even for a short period, irreparable engine damage is inevitable.

54 Fault diagnosis: engine

Symptom	Cause	Remedy
Engine will not start	Defective spark plugs	Remove the plugs and lay them on the cylinder head. Check whether spark occurs when ignition is on and engine rotated.
	Dirty or closed contact breaker points	Check the condition of the points and whether the points gap is correct.
	Faulty or disconnected condenser	Check whether the points arc when separated. Renew the condenser if there is evidence of arcing.
Engine runs unevenly	Ignition or fuel system fault	Check each system independently, as though engine will not start.
	Blowing cylinder head gasket	Leak should be evident from oil leakage where gas escapes.
	Incorrect ignition timing	Check accuracy and reset if necessary.
Lack of power	Fault in fuel system or incorrect ignition timing	Check fuel lines or float chambers for sediment. Reset ignition timing.
Heavy oil consumption	Cylinder block in need of rebore	Check bore wear; rebore and fit oversize pistons if required.

55 Fault diagnosis: gearbox

Symptom	Cause	Remedy
Difficulty in engaging gears	Selector forks bent	Replace with new forks.
	Gear clusters not assembled correctly	Check gear cluster for arrangement and position of thrust washers.
Machine jumps out of gear	Worn dogs on the ends of gear pinions	Renew worn pinions.
Gear change lever does not return to original position	Broken return spring	Renew spring.
Kickstart does not return when engine is turned over or started	Broken or wrongly tensioned return spring	Renew spring or retension.
Kickstart slips	Ratchet assembly worn	Dismantle gearbox and replace all worn parts.

56 Fault diagnosis: clutch

Symptom	Cause	Remedy
Engine speed increases as shown by tachometer but machine does not respond	Clutch slip	Check clutch adjustment for free play, at handlebar lever, check thickness of inserted plates.
Difficulty in engaging gears, gear changes jerky and machine creeps forward when clutch is withdrawn, difficulty in selecting neutral	Clutch drag	Check clutch for too much free-play. Check plates for burrs on tongues or drum for indentations. Dress with file if damage not too great.
Clutch operation stiff	Damaged, trapped or frayed control cable.	Check cable and replace if necessary. Make sure cable is lubricated and has no sharp bends.

Chapter 2 Fuel system and lubrication

Contents

Specifications

Petrol tank
Capacity	14 lit (3.7/3.1 US/Imp gal)
Reserve	1.6 lit (3.4/2.8 US/Imp pint)

Carburettors
Make	Mikuni
Type	BS34
Main jet	112.5 (110, 400C model)
Air jet	0.6
Needle jet	Y-O
Jet needle (piston needle)	AF23-3
Pilot jet	20
Pilot air jet	1.3
Piston spring:	
Tension	154 ± 10 g (0.34 ± 0.02 lb)
Length	60.8 mm (2.39 in)
Pilot air screw: no of turns out	$\frac{3}{4} - 1\frac{1}{4}$
Float level	26.3 ± 1.0 mm (1.035 ± 0.039 in)

Engine oil capacity .... 2.1 lit (4.4/3.6 US/Imp pint)
Oil specifications	SAE 10W/40 or 20W/50
Oil pump	
Inner/Outer rotor clearance (max)	0.20 mm (0.008 in)
Outer rotor/body clearance (max)	0.25 mm (0.0098 in)
Side clearance (max)	0.15 mm (0.0059 in)
Oil pump pressure	over 0.3 kg/cm² (4.3 psi) at 3000 rpm at 60°C (140°F)

1 General description

The fuel system comprises a petrol tank from which petrol is fed by gravity to the float chamber of each of the two carburettors. A single petrol tap with a detachable gauze filter is located beneath the petrol tank, on the left-hand side. It contains provision for a reserve quantity of petrol, when the main supply is exhausted.

In both the ON and RES positions, fuel can only flow to the carburettors when the engine is running. This is due to the tap diaphragm which is controlled by the induction pressure. If there is no fuel in the float chambers, as may be the case after carburettor dismantling, the petrol tap should be turned to the PRIMING position, to allow an unrestricted flow of petrol to the float chambers. Return the tap to the ON position as soon as the engine is running.

Two constant velocity (CV) Mikuni carburettors are fitted, mounted on an aluminium alloy bracket as a unit. The carburettors are controlled by an opening and a closing cable which pass over a pulley mounted on a cross-shaft to operate the throttle butterfly valves.

For cold starting, a hand-operated choke lever attached to the far left-hand carburettor is linked to the right-hand carburettor, so that the mixture can be enriched temporarily. When the engine has started, the choke can be opened gradually as the engine warms up, until full air is accepted under normal running conditions.

Lubrication is effected by the wet sump principle in which the reservoir of oil is contained within engine sump. This oil is shared by the engine, primary drive and transmission components. The oil pump is of the Eaton trochoid type and is driven from a pinion engaged with and to the rear of the clutch.

Oil is supplied under pressure, via a full flow oil filter with a replaceable element, to the crankshaft and to the overhead camshaft and rocker gear. A secondary flow passes to the gearbox via the gearbox main bearings. All surplus oil drains to the sump and is returned to the oil tank by the scavenge section of the oil pump. The pump itself is protected by a gauze strainer in the base of the oil pick-up funnel.

2 Petrol tank: removal and replacement

1 The petrol tank is retained by two guide channels which locate with a circular rubber block on each side of the steering head and a bolt passing through a lug at the rear of the tank and into the frame.

2 To remove the tank, leave the petrol tap lever at the On or Reserve position and detach the diaphragm vacuum pipe and the larger bore petrol feed pipe. The latter pipe is secured at the union by a spring clip, the ears of which should be pinched together to release the tension on the pipe. Remove the bolt from the rear of the tank, after raising the dualseat to gain access.

3 Lift the tank up at the rear and then ease the unit backwards until the location cups leave the rubber blocks. Lift the tank upwards off the machine.

4 Drainage of petrol is not strictly necessary when removing the tank, although the reduction in weight will facilitate the operation. A full tank weighs approximately 50 lbs.

5 Replace the petrol tank by reversing the removal procedure. Take care not to trap control cables or stray wires between the tank and frame tubes. If the cups are a tight fit on the rubber blocks, apply a small amount of washing-up detergent to the blocks to ease refitting.

3 Petrol tap: removal and replacement

1 Removal of the complete petrol tap is required at regular intervals to gain access to the filter columns for cleaning. The

tank should be drained of petrol by fitting a length of tubing to the petrol tap outlet and turning the lever to the Priming position.

2 The petrol tap is held to the underside of the petrol tank by two crosshead screws with washers. Note that there is an 'O' ring seal between the petrol tap body and the petrol tank, which must be renewed if it is damaged or if petrol leakage has occurred. The filter screens which are integral with the plastic level pipes should be cleaned of any deposits using a soft brush and clean petrol. Because there is only a single tap to feed two carburettors, any restriction in petrol flow may lead to fuel starvation, causing missing and in extreme cases overheating, due to a weak mixture.

3 It is seldom necessary to remove the lever which operates the petrol tap, although occasions may occur when a leakage develops at the joint. Although the tank must be drained before the lever assembly can be removed, there is no need to disturb the body of the tap.

4 To dismantle the lever assembly, remove the two crosshead screws passing through the plate on which the operating positions are inscribed. The plate can then be lifted away, followed by a spring, the lever itself and the seal behind the lever. The seal will have to be renewed if leakage has occurred. Reassemble the tap in the reverse order. Gasket cement or any other sealing medium is NOT necessary to secure a petrol tight seal.

4 Carburettors: removal from the machine

1 To improve access to the carburettors it is suggested that the petrol tank is removed, as described in Section 2 of this Chapter, before dismantling proper commences.

2 Detach the engine breather hose from the unions at the air filter box and the breather cover on the cylinder head. The hose is secured at both ends by spring clips.

3 Loosen the screw clips which secure the air filter hoses and inlet stubs to the carburettors.

To gain sufficient clearance for carburettor removal, the inlet stubs must be detached from the cylinder head and removed together with the two insulation blocks. Each stub and block is secured by two bolts. Pull the carburettors forwards, away from the air hoses, and then out towards the right-hand side of the machine.

4 Disconnect the throttle cables from the operating pulley at the carburettors. Both may be detached in a similar manner. Loosen the upper and lower locknuts on the cable adjuster screw and displace the adjuster and outer cable from the abutment bracket. Rotate the pulley until the inner cable nipple can be pushed out of the anchor point.

3.2 Petrol tap filter may be cleaned in petrol using soft brush

3.4 Lever assembly is held by two screws

5   Carburettors: dismantling and reassembly

1   The carburettors are mounted as a unit on an aluminium bracket and are interconnected by the throttle link and the choke control rod. Before the dismantling of each individual carburettor is commenced, the two instruments must be separated by removal from the bracket.

2   Remove the pivot screw securing the choke lever. Detach the lever, noting carefully the sequence of washers. Slacken the grub screw holding each choke plunger operating fork. The choke link rod can now be withdrawn, freeing the forks. Slacken the four screws which secure the top to each carburettor, and then remove the inner two screws from each instrument, to free the top bracket. Invert the instruments and remove the four screws which retain the mounting bracket. Take especial care when loosening these screws because they are usually very tight. The carburettors are now connected only by the fuel cross-over pipe. Pull the two instruments apart. Dismantle each carburettor separately, to prevent accidental interchange of parts.

3   Remove the drain plug from the base of the float chamber to gain access to the main jet. Using a close fitting screwdriver, unscrew the jet.

4   Remove the four screws which secure the float chamber to the main body and lift the chamber away, taking care not to damage the gasket. The pilot jet is screwed into the inside of the float chamber.

5   Remove the hinge pin that locates the twin float assembly and lift away the float. This will expose the float needle. The needle is very small and should be put in a safe place so that it is not misplaced.

6   Make sure the float chamber gasket is in good condition. It should not be disturbed unless it shows sign of damage or has been leaking.

7   Pull out the push fit needle jet from the centre of the main body roof, noting the small 'O' ring.

8   Invert the carburettor and remove the two remaining screws which secure the carburettor top. Lift out the piston spring, followed by the piston/diaphragm unit together with the needle. Invert the piston to allow the needle and needle seat to drop out.

9   The starter plunger (choke) assembly is housed within a detachable casing retained on one side of the carburettor by three screws. The plunger may be displaced after unscrewing the housing nut. Attention to the choke is rarely required as wear is limited.

10   It is not recommended that the 'butterfly' throttle valve assembly be removed as these components are not prone to wear. If wear occurs on the operating pivot a new carburettor will be required as air will find its way along the pivot bearings resulting in a weak mixture.

11   Check the condition of the floats. If they are damaged in any way, they should be renewed. The float needle and needle seating will wear after lengthy service and should be inspected carefully. Wear usually takes the form of a ridge or groove, which will cause the float needle to seat imperfectly. Always renew the seating and needle as a pair. An imperfection in one component will soon produce similar wear in the other.

12   After considerable service the piston needle and the needle jet in which it slides will wear, resulting in an increase in petrol consumption. Wear is caused by the passage of petrol and the two components rubbing together. It is advisable to renew the jet periodically in conjunction with the piston needle. Check the diaphragm for signs of perishing or for splits. If damage is evident the diaphragm must be renewed as a unit with the piston.

13   Before the carburettors are reassembled, using the reversed dismantling procedure, each should be cleaned out thoroughly using compressed air. Avoid using a piece of rag since there is always risk of particles of lint obstructing the internal passage ways or the jet orifices.

14   Never use a piece of wire or any pointed metal object to clear a blocked jet. It is only too easy to enlarge the jet under these circumstances and increase the rate of petrol consumption. If compressed air is not available, a blast of air from a tyre pump will usually suffice.

15   Do not use excessive force when reassembling a carburettor because it is easy to shear a jet or some of the smaller screws. Furthermore, the carburettors are cast in a zinc-based alloy which itself does not have a high tensile strength. Take particular care when replacing the pistons to ensure the needles align with the jet seats. Note that the rubber diaphragm has two location projections, these must be aligned with the recesses in the carburettor on re-installation.

16   Do NOT remove either the throttle stop screw or the pilot jet screw without first making note of their exact positions. Failure to observe this precaution will make it necessary to re-synchronise both carburettors on reassembly.

17   When refitting the two instruments to the mounting box, check that the fuel cross-over pipe is in good condition and is a tight fit on the union bosses. The throttle link arm on the right-hand instrument should engage the opposing throttle arm so that it lies between the spring loaded plunger and the throttle valve synchronisation screw.

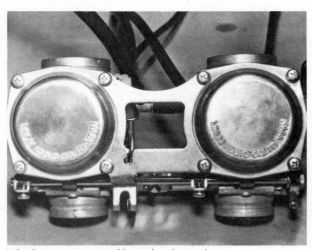

5.2a Remove upper and lower bracket and ...

5.2b ... slacken choke arm screws to allow ...

5.2c ... separation of the two instruments

5.3a Remove float bowl drain plug to ...

5.3b ... gain access to main jet

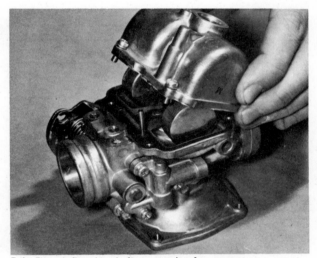

5.4a Detach float bowl after removing four screws

5.4b Unscrew pilot jet from inside the float bowl

5.5a Slide out pivot pin to free float unit

5.5b Tiny float needle is easy to mislay

5.7 Needle jet

5.8a Lift off carburettor top after removing remaining screws

5.8b Pull out piston/diaphragm unit and ...

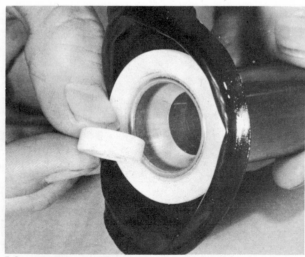

5.8c ... displace needle seat and ...

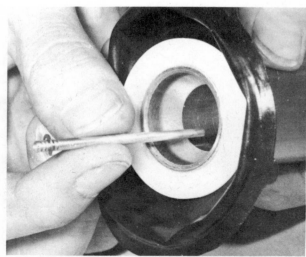

5.8d ... piston needle

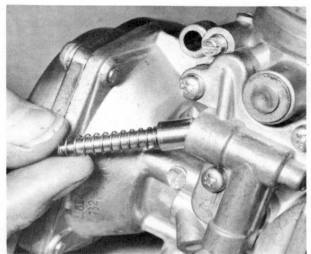

5.9a Starter plunger (choke) can be pulled out after ...

5.9b ... unscrewing housing cap

5.11a Note filter which can be cleaned after ...

5.11b ... removal of float needle seat

5.15 Projections on diaphragm must locate with recesses

5.17 Throttle link arm should be inserted between spring and plunger

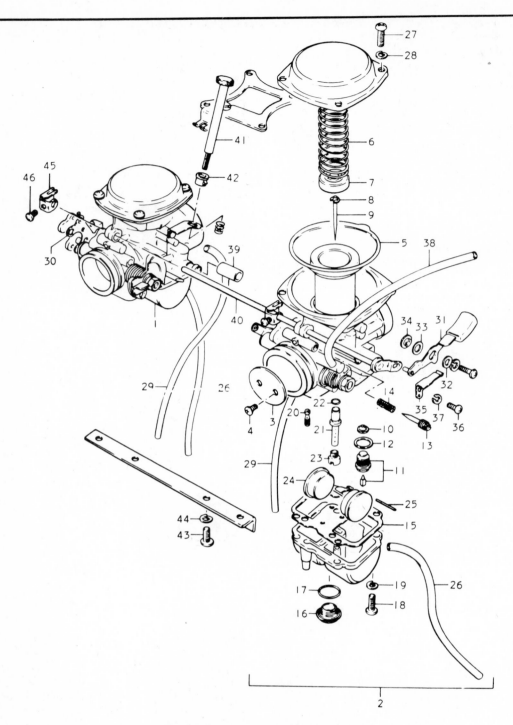

Fig. 2.1 Carburettors – component parts

1 RH carburettor	12 Sealing washer – 2 off	24 Float assembly – 2 off	36 Screw
2 LH carburettor	13 Pilot air screw – 2 off	25 Float pivot pin – 2 off	37 Spring washer
3 Throttle butterfly valve – 2 off	14 Spring – 2 off	26 Breather hose – 2 off	38 Fuel pipe
4 Screws – 4 off	15 Float chamber gasket	27 Screw – 8 off	39 Transfer pipe
5 Piston/diaphragm – 2 off	16 Drain plug – 2 off	28 Spring washer – 8 off	40 Choke link rod
6 Spring – 2 off	17 'O' ring – 2 off	29 Hose – 2 off	41 Throttle stop screw
7 Needle seat – 2 off	18 Screw – 8 off	30 Gasket	42 Bush
8 Needle clip – 2 off	19 Spring washer – 8 off	31 Choke lever	43 Screw – 4 off
9 Jet needle – 2 off	20 Pilot jet – 2 off	32 Plain washer	44 Spring washer – 4 off
10 Filter – 2 off	21 Needle jet – 2 off	33 Plain washer	45 Choke arm – 2 off
11 Float valve assembly – 2 off	22 'O' ring – 2 off	34 Special washer	46 Grub screw – 2 off
	23 Main jet – 2 off	35 Spring plate	

6 Carburettors: synchronisation and adjustment

1 Synchonisation and adjustment of the carburettors should be carried out as a routine maintenance item. It may also be necessary when rough idling or poor performance is encountered and also after dismantling and reassembly has taken place. The procedure for these adjustments is made in two stages. The first stage is adjustment of the tick-over (idle) speed and mixture strength, by means of the shared throttle stop screw and the pilot screws respectively. The second stage, which is the synchronisation of the two carburettors, requires the use of two vacuum gauges together with the necessary adaptors and connection tubes. Vacuum gauges are somewhat expensive. For this reason, and because both stages of adjustment require some expertise, it is strongly recommended that the machine is returned to a Suzuki Service Agent who will be able to carry out the work for a small fee.

Incorrect carburettor adjustment will affect performance and fuel economy adversely and may, in extreme cases, cause overheating problems. In addition, injudicious attention to the carburettors may prevent the machine from complying with certain emission regulations currently in force in some areas.

2 Before carrying out adjustments of the carburettors, it is important to check that the following items are adjusted correctly; valve clearance, contact breaker gap, ignition timing and spark plug gap. Many developing engine faults which at first are thought to be due to carburettor maladjustment can often be traced to those components listed above. The ignition system and timing are particularly prone to this.

3 Both stages of adjustment **must** be carried out with the engine at normal working temperature, preferably after the machine has been taken for a short run.

Start the engine and by means of the nylon headed throttle stop screw located between the two instruments set the engine tick-over speed to within the range 1,100 – 1,200 rpm. The mixture strength must now be adjusted on each carburettor in turn. Select one carburettor and screw in the pilot screw fully until it can be felt to seat lightly. **Do not overtighten** because the screw may break. Now unscrew the pilot screw one full turn. Rotate the screw first clockwise then anti-clockwise from this position, no more than a $\frac{1}{4}$ of a turn in each direction until the position is found where the engine is running at highest speed. This position must be between $\frac{3}{4}$ and $1\frac{1}{4}$ turns out. With the engine running at the highest speed within the specified range, the pilot adjustment for the carburettor in question is now correct. Repeat the procedure on the second carburettor and then readjust the tick-over to the specified speed.

4 Synchronisation of the two carburettors, as mentioned above, requires the use of a pair of vacuum gauges and the correct adaptors for interconnection with the inlet tracts. If the necessary equipment is available, it should be connected up, following the manufacturer's recommendations. A blanking plug in the form of a socket screw is fitted to each side of the cylinder, just forward of the inlet stub flange. After removal of these, the adaptors may be fitted.

Start the engine and set the speed to 1750 rpm. If the gauge readings differ, rotate the throttle valve link adjuster screw either anti-clockwise or clockwise until the two readings are equal. The carburettors are now synchronised.

7 Carburettors: checking the float chamber fuel level

1 If conditions of a continual weak mixture or flooding are encountered on one or other carburettor or if difficulty is experienced in tuning the carburettors, the float levels should be checked, and if necessary, adjusted. Although the float chambers may be removed with the carburettors in-situ on the machine it is advised that the carburettors be removed to facilitate inspection and adjustment.

2 The float level is correct when the distance between the uppermost edge of the floats (with the carburettor inverted) and the mixing chamber body flange is 26·3 $\pm$ 1 mm (1·035 $\pm$ 0·039 in); the gasket must be removed from the mixing chamber body before the measurement is taken. The needle valve should be just in the closed position when the measurement is taken. Adjustment is made by bending the float assembly tang (tongue), which engages with the float, in the direction required.

8 Carburettors: settings

1 Some of the carburettor settings, such as the sizes of the needle jets, main jets, and needle positions are pre-determined by the manufacturer. Under normal riding conditions it is unlikely that these settings will require modification. If a change appears necessary, it is often because of an engine fault, or an alteration in the exhaust system eg; a leaky exhaust pipe connection or silencer.

2 Apart from alterations of the pilot adjuster screws within the specified limits, some alterations to the mid-range mixture strength may be made by raising or lowering the jet needle (piston needle). This is accomplished by changing the position of the needle clip. Raising the needle will richen the mixture and lowering the needle will weaken it.

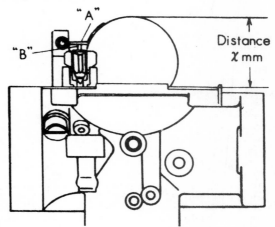

Fig. 2.2 Checking float level

A – Float tongue
B – Float valve
X – 26.3 $\pm$ 1 mm (1.035 $\pm$ 0.030 in)

6.1a A = shared throttle stop screw, B = throttle synchronisation screw

6.1b Pilot adjustment screw

8.2 Jet needle clip may be raised or lowered to alter mixture

9   Air cleaner: dismantling, servicing and reassembly

1   The air cleaner is mounted immediately behind the carburettors. The air filter housing contains the element that is removable for cleaning or replacement, when necessary.

2   To gain access to the air filter element raise the dualseat and remove the air filter box lid, which is secured by two screws. The air filter element and carrier can be lifted out after removal of the single carrier screw.

3   Detach the air filter element by displacing the spring-steel strip. The element is of oil impregnated polyurethane sponge and should be cleaned thoroughly in petrol to remove all the old oil and dust. After cleaning, squeeze out the sponge to remove the petrol and then allow a short time for the remaining petrol to evaporate. Do not wring out the sponge as this will cause damage and will lead to the need for early renewal. Reimpregnate the sponge with engine oil and gently squeeze out the excess.

4   Reinstall the element and carrier by reversing the removal procedure.

5   The air filter should be removed for cleaning at approximately 3000 mile intervals. If the sponge becomes damaged or hardened with age, it should be renewed as a matter of course. Never run the machine without the element or with the air cleaner disconnected, otherwise the weak mixture that results will cause engine overheating and severe damage.

10   Engine and gearbox lubrication

1   As previously described at the beginning of the Chapter the lubrication system is of the wet sump type, with the oil being forceably pumped from the sump to positions at the gearbox bearings, the main engine bearings, and the cambox bearings, all oil eventually draining back to the sump. The system incorporates a gear driven oil pump, an oil filter and a safety by-pass valve. Oil vapours created in the crankcase are vented through a breather to the air cleaner box, where they are passed into the cylinder providing an oiltight system.

2   The oil pump is an Eaton trochoid twin rotor unit which is driven from a gear engaged with and to the rear of the clutch. An oil strainer is fitted to the intake side of the pump, which serves to protect the pump mechanism from impurities in the oil which might cause damage.

3   A corrugated paper oil filter is included in the system and is

fitted within an enclosed chamber on the underside of the crankcase. Access to the filter is made through a finned cover. As the oil filter unit becomes clogged with impurities, its ability to function correctly is reduced, and if it becomes so clogged that it begins to impede the oil flow, a by-pass valve opens, and routes the oil flow through the filter core. This results in unfiltered oil being circulated throughout the engine, a condition which is avoided if the filter element is changed at regular intervals.

4   As previously mentioned, an oil breather is incorporated into the system. It is mounted in the top of the camshaft cover and is essential for an engine of this size with so many moving parts. It serves to minimise crankcase pressure variations due piston and crankshaft movement, and also helps lower the oil temperature, by venting the crankcase. Furthermore, this system reduces the escape of unburnt oil into the atmosphere and so allows use of the machine in countries where stringent anti-pollution statutes are in operation. The breather tube carries the crankcase vapours to the air cleaner housing where they become mixed with the air drawn into the carburettors.

5   Excessive oil consumption is indicated by blue smoke being emitted from the exhaust pipes, coupled with a poor performance and fouling of spark plugs. It is caused by either an excessive oil build-up in the oil breather chamber, or by oil getting past the piston rings. First check the oil breather chamber and air cleaner for oil sludge build-up. If this is the fault, check the passageway from the air/oil separator in the oil breather chamber to the lower half of the crankcase. Blockage here will prevent oil flowing back into the crankcase, resulting in oil build-up in the breather chamber and air cleaner tube.

6   Be sure to check the oil level in the sump before starting the engine. If the oil level is not seen between the two marks adjacent to the sight window at the bottom of the clutch cover, replenish with the correct amount of oil of the specified viscosity.

11   Oil pump: removal and examination

1   The oil pump is secured to the wall of the primary drive chamber behind the clutch unit. To gain access to the pump, the engine oil should be drained and the primary drive cover detached. The clutch should then be removed as described in Chapter 1, Section 10 paragraphs 1–4.

2   Unscrew the three screws retaining the oil pump and lift it from position. Displace the two 'O' rings in the casing wall. The oil pump pinion is retained on the pump shaft. Remove the circlip, lift the pinion off the shaft and push out the drive pin.

3   Remove the single screw from the reverse side of the pump body. The two halves of the pump body are located by two tight fitting dowel pins. Rather than levering the cases apart, which would damage the mating surfaces, the dowels should be driven out. Use a parallel shanked punch of a suitable size, whilst resting the pump across two strips of wood of a thickness sufficient to raise the pump off the workbench surface.

4   Separate the outer casing (reverse side) from the pump, leaving the drive shaft and rotors in place at this stage. Push out the drive shaft, together with the drive pin and then lift out the two rotors.

5   Wash all the pump components with petrol and allow them to dry before carrying out a full examination. Before part reassembling the pump for the various measurements to be made, check the castings for cracks or other damage, especially the pump end covers.

6   Reassemble the pump rotors and measure the clearance between the outer rotor and the pump body, using a feeler gauge. If the clearance exceeds 0·25 mm (0·0098 in) the rotor or the body must be renewed, whichever is worn. Measure the clearance between the outer rotor and the inner rotor with a feeler gauge. If this clearance is greater than 0·2 mm (0·008 in) the rotors must be renewed as a set.

7   Using a small sheet of plate glass or a straight edge placed across the pump housing, check the rotor endfloat. If the end-float exceeds 0·15 mm 0·006 in) the complete pump must be renewed.

8   Examine the rotors and the pump body for signs of scoring, chipping or other surface damage which will occur if metallic particles find their way into the oil pump assembly. Renewal of the affected parts is the only remedy under these circumstances, bearing in mind that rotors must always be replaced as a matched set.

9   Reassemble the pump by reversing the dismantling procedure. Make sure all parts of the pump are well lubricated before the end cover is replaced and that there is plenty of oil between the inner and outer rotors. Apply a small quantity of locking fluid to the thread of the single casing screw. **Do not** omit the two 'O' rings when fitting the oil pump into the casing. Rotate the drive shaft as the screws are tightened down, to check that the oil pump revolves freely. A binding pump may be caused by dirt on the rotor faces or distortion of the cases, due to unequally tightened screws.

9.2a Remove air filter cover held by two screws to enable ...

9.2b ... air filter element to be lifted out

11.2a Displace circlip to free oil pump pinion

11.2b Note drive pin passing through shaft

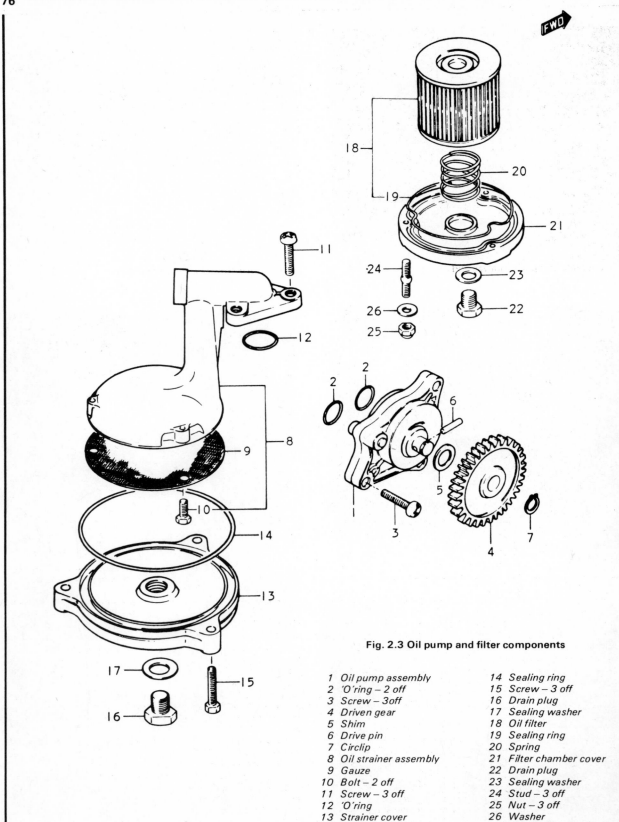

Fig. 2.3 Oil pump and filter components

1	Oil pump assembly	14	Sealing ring
2	'O' ring – 2 off	15	Screw – 3 off
3	Screw – 3off	16	Drain plug
4	Driven gear	17	Sealing washer
5	Shim	18	Oil filter
6	Drive pin	19	Sealing ring
7	Circlip	20	Spring
8	Oil strainer assembly	21	Filter chamber cover
9	Gauze	22	Drain plug
10	Bolt – 2 off	23	Sealing washer
11	Screw – 3 off	24	Stud – 3 off
12	'O' ring	25	Nut – 3 off
13	Strainer cover	26	Washer

11.3a Separate pump body halves and ...

11.3b ... push out drive shaft and inner pin

11.6a Measure outer rotor/body clearance and ...

11.6b ... outer rotor/inner rotor clearance, using a feeler gauge

12 Checking the oil pressure

1   Because of the predominant use of caged ball and roller bearings in the GS series of engines, a low pressure lubrication system is employed. If the condition of the oil pump is suspect, the output pressure may be checked by connecting a suitable pressure gauge to the engine.

2   A blanking plug is fitted to the left-hand end of the main oil passage which runs across the crankcase below and to the rear of the cylinder block. The blanking plug should be substituted by a suitable adaptor piece to which the pressure gauge can be attached, via a flexible hose.

3   After connection of the pressure gauge, check that the oil level in the crankcase is correct and then start the engine. The engine should be run until the oil is at approximately 60°C (140°F). Raise the engine speed to 3000 rpm, when the pressure gauge should give a reading of 0·3 – 0·38 kg cm² (4·27 – 5·40 psi). It can be seen that the pressure gauge must be of high sensitivity and of the correct calibration to give a useful reading. A pressure reading lower than specified may be caused by a worn oil pump, a blocked oil strainer or oil filter element. Before dismantling the pump for inspection, clean the oil strainer and renew the oil filter, as described in Section 13 of this Chapter.

13 Oil filter and gauze strainer: renewing the element and cleaning the strainer

1   The oil filter element is contained within a semi-isolated chamber in the base of the lower crankcase, closed by a finned cover retained by three domed nuts. To the rear of the oil filter cover is a second cover which encloses the oil strainer gauze fitted to the oil pick-up funnel (early models only). On later models access to the gauze can be made only during an overhaul as no cover is fitted.

2   Before removing the oil filter cover, place a receptacle below the engine to catch the engine oil contained within the filter chamber. Drain the oil either by removing the drain plug provided or by releasing the cover.

A coil spring is fitted between the cover and the filter element to keep the latter seated firmly in position. Be prepared for the cover to fly off after removal of the bolts.

No attempt should be made to clean the oil filter element; it must be renewed. When renewing the filter element it is wise to renew the filter cover 'O' ring at the same time. This will obviate the possibility of any oil leaks.

3   The by-pass valve, which allows a continued flow of lubrication if the element becomes clogged, is an integral part of the filter. For this reason routine cleaning of the valve is not required since it is renewed regularly.

4   Never run the engine without the filter element or increase the period between the recommended oil changes or oil filter changes. The oil should be changed every 1500 miles and the oil filter renewed at every second oil change.

5   The oil pick-up strainer gauze should be removed at intervals of approximately 6000 miles (every fourth oil change) for cleaning. Access to the strainer is gained by removal of the forward cover, secured to the underside of the crankcase by three bolts. To detach the strainer remove the two screws and twist the unit anti-clockwise a few degrees. The obscured rear edge of the strainer is located by a bent tang which engages with the funnel mouth periphery. The strainer gauze may be cleaned in petrol, using a soft brush.

6   When refitting the strainer ensure that the securing tang locates correctly at the rear of the funnel. Check that the cover gasket is in good condition before refitting the cover.

13.1 The finned cover encloses oil filter element

13.5a Remove rear cover to gain access to ...

13.5b ... oil strainer, which is secured by two bolts

14 Fault diagnosis: fuel system and lubrication

Symptom	Cause	Remedy
Engine gradually fades and stops	Fuel starvation	Check vent hole in filler cap. Sediment in filter bowl or float chamber. Dismantle and clean.
Engine runs badly. Black smoke from exhausts	Carburettor flooding	Dismantle and clean carburettor. Check for punctured float or sticking float needle.
Engine lacks response and overheats	Weak mixture Air cleaner disconnected or hose split Modified silencer has upset carburation	Check for partial block in carburettors. Reconnect or renew hose. Replace with original design.
Oil pressure warning light comes on	Lubrication system failure	Stop engine immediately. Trace and rectify fault before re-starting.
Engine gets noisy	Failure to change engine oil when recommended	Drain off old oil and refill with new oil of correct grade. Renew oil filter element.

Chapter 3 Ignition system

Contents

Specifications

Contact breaker
Points gap .... 0·3 – 0·4 mm (0·012 – 0·016 in)

Ignition timing
Retarded .... 10° BTDC
Fully advanced .... 40° BTDC
Advance commences .... 1500 rpm
Advance completed .... 3600 rpm

Condenser
Capacity: Kokusan .... 0·25 microFarads
         Denso .... 0·18 microFarads

Spark plugs

	NGK*	Nippon Denso*	Motocraft
Make			
Type	B–8ES	W24ES	AG1
Gap	0·6 – 0·7 mm (0·024 – 0·028 in)		

*Manufacturers recommendation

---

1 General description

1   The spark necessary to ignite the petrol/air mixture in the combustion chambers is derived from the alternator attached to the left-hand end of the crankshaft. A twin contact breaker assembly, one set of points for each cylinder, determines the exact moment at which the spark will occur in the cylinder that is due to fire. As the points separate, the low tension circuit is interrupted and a high tension voltage is developed in the ignition coil, which passes across the points of the spark plug due to fire. This jumps the air gap and ignites the mixture under compression.

2   When the engine is running, the surplus current generated by the alternator is used to provide a regulated 12 volt supply for charging the battery, after it has been converted to direct current by the rectifier. The output from the alternator is con-trolled by a silicon-controlled regulator (SCR unit) to within a preset range. Excess current is passed to earth to prevent output rising above the specified maximum level.

2 Crankshaft alternator: checking the output

1   If the charging performance of the alternator is suspect, it can be checked with a multi-meter test instrument that includes a voltmeter and ohmmeter. As most owner/riders are unlikely to possess equipment of this type it is advised that the machine be returned to a Suzuki Service Agent for testing.

2   If a multi-meter is available, an initial check on the alter-nator and the rectifier and regulator assemblies may be carried out as described in Chapter 6. As mentioned in Chapter 6, Section 3, the charging system should be considered as a whole, and should be testing accordingly.

3 Ignition coils: checking

1   Each ignition coil is a sealed unit, designed to give long service without need for attention. They are located within the top frame tubes, immediately to the rear of the steering head assembly. If a weak spark and difficult starting causes the performance of a coil to be suspect, it should be tested by a Suzuki Service Agent or an auto-electrical engineer who will have the appropriate test equipment. A faulty coil must be renewed; it is not possible to effect a satisfactory repair.

2   A defective condenser in the contact breaker circuit can give the illusion of a defective coil and for this reason it is advisable to investigate the condition of the condenser before condemning the ignition coil. Refer to Section 6 of this Chapter for the appropriate details.

3   Note that it is extremely unlikely that both ignition coils will prove faulty at the same time, unless the common electrical feed is in some way deranged. This can be checked by measuring the low tension voltage supplied to the coils, using a voltmeter.

4 Contact breaker: adjustments

1   To gain access to the contact breaker assembly, it is necessary to detach the aluminium cover retained by three crosshead screws at the right-hand end of the crankshaft. Note that the cover has a sealing gasket, to prevent the ingress of water.

2   Rotate the engine slowly by means of the engine turning hexagon until one set of points is in the fully open position. Examine the faces of the contacts. If they are blackened and burnt, or badly pitted, it will be necessary to remove them for further attention. See Section 5 of this Chapter. Repeat for the second set of contact points.

3   Adjustment is effected by slackening the screw through the plate of the fixed contact breaker point and moving the point either closer to or further from the moving contact until the gap is correct as measured by a feeler gauge. The correct gap with the points FULLY OPEN is 0·3 – 0·4 mm (0·012 – 0·016 in). Small projections on the contact breaker baseplate permit the insertion of a screwdriver to lever the adjustable point into its correct location. Repeat this operation for the second set of points, which must also be fully open.

4   Do NOT slacken the two screws through the extremities of the larger baseplate fitted to the right-hand set of contact breaker points. They are used for adjusting the setting of the ignition timing and it will be necessary to re-time the engine if the baseplate is permitted to move. Only the centre screw should be slackened, to adjust the fixed contact breaker point.

5   Before replacing the cover and gasket, place a light smear of grease on the contact breaker cam and one or two drops of thin oil on the felt which lubricates the surface of the cam. It is better to under-lubricate rather than add excess because there is always chance of excess oil reaching the contact breaker points and causing the ignition circuit to malfunction.

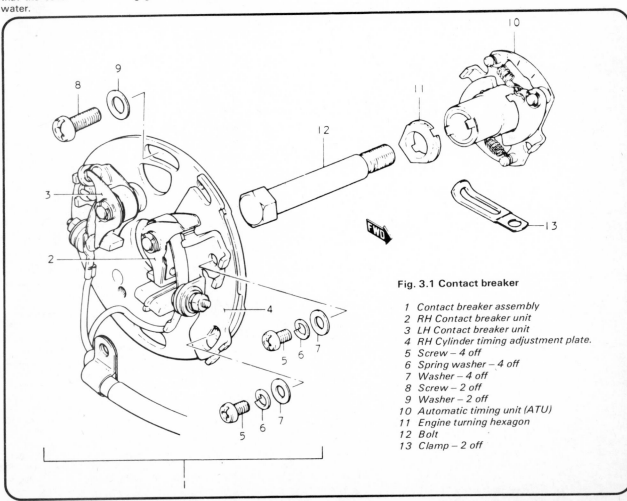

Fig. 3.1 Contact breaker

1 Contact breaker assembly
2 RH Contact breaker unit
3 LH Contact breaker unit
4 RH Cylinder timing adjustment plate.
5 Screw – 4 off
6 Spring washer – 4 off
7 Washer – 4 off
8 Screw – 2 off
9 Washer – 2 off
10 Automatic timing unit (ATU)
11 Engine turning hexagon
12 Bolt
13 Clamp – 2 off

5 Contact breaker points: removal, renovation and replacement

1 If the contact breaker points are burned, pitted or badly worn, they should be removed for dressing. If it is necessary to remove a substantial amount of material before the faces can be restored, the points should be renewed.

2 To remove the contact breaker points, detach the circlip which secures the moving contact to the pin on which it pivots. Remove the nut and bolt which secures the flexible lead wire to the end of contact return spring, noting the arrangement of the insulating washers so that they are replaced in their correct order during reassembly. Lift the moving contact off the pivot, away from the assembly.

3 The fixed contact is removed by unscrewing the screw which retains the contact to the contact breaker baseplate.

4 The points should be dressed with an oilstone or fine emery cloth. Keep them absolutely square throughout the dressing operation, otherwise they will make angular contact on reassembly, and rapidly burn away.

5 Replace the contacts by reversing the dismantling procedure, making sure that the insulating washers are fitted in the correct order. It is advantageous to apply a thin smear of grease to the pivot pin, prior to replacement of the moving contact arm.

6 Check, and if necessary, re-adjust the contact breaker gap when the points are fully open. Repeat the whole operation for the second set of points.

6 Condensers: removal and replacement

1 A condenser is included in each contact breaker circuit to prevent arcing across the contact breaker points as they separate. It is connected in parallel with each set of points and if a fault develops, ignition failure is liable to occur.

2 If the engine proves difficult to start, or misfiring occurs, it is possible that the condenser is at fault. To check, separate the contact breaker points by hand when the ignition is switched on. If a spark occurs across the points and they have a blackened and burnt appearance, the condenser can be regarded as unserviceable.

3 It is not possible to check a condenser without the appropriate test equipment. In view of the low cost involved, it is preferable to fit a new one and observe the effect on engine performance.

4 Because each condenser has its associated set of contact breaker points, a faulty condenser will cause a misfire on one cylinder only. It follows that both condensers are unlikely to fail at the same time unless damaged in an accident. If the cases are crushed or dented, electrical breakdown will occur.

5 The two condensers are mounted behind the ignition coils, one condenser being attached to each coil. In the case of failure the petrol tank must be removed to gain access.

7 Ignition timing: checking and resetting

1 In order to check the accuracy of the ignition timing, it is necessary to remove the contact breaker cover from the right-hand side of the crankcase. Ignition timing checking and resetting should take place after resetting the contact breaker gaps, as described in Section 4.

2 Apply a spanner to the engine rotation hexagon and turn the engine in a forward direction, whilst viewing the ATU through the inspection aperture in the contact breaker stator plate. It will be seen that there is a set of three scribed lines on each side of the ATU. Each side is marked 'R' or 'L' to differentiate which marks control which cylinder.

3 Commence ignition timing checking on the left-hand contact breaker set, which controls the left-hand cylinder. To determine at which moment the points open, connect a 12v bulb between the moving point and a suitable earthing point on the engine. With the ignition turned on, the bulb will light up when the points are open. Rotate the engine until the F mark on the left-hand side of the ATU is in **exact** alignment with the index pointer mark on the casing to the rear of the stator plate. If the ignition is correct, the points should be on the verge of opening when this position is reached. This will be indicated by the flickering of the bulb.

4 To adjust the ignition timing on the left-hand cylinder slacken the three screws which pass through the elongated holes in the stator plate periphery. Rotate the plate until the light flickers and then tighten the screws. Turn the engine backwards about 90° and then forwards again to check the setting.

5 Check the ignition timing on right-hand cylinder in a similar manner, using the F – R (right-hand) timing mark on the ATU. If the timing is incorrect, slacken the two screws holding the right-hand contact breaker assembly mounting plate to the main stator plate. Move the plate to the correct position and tighten the screws. **Do not** slacken the three stator plate screws because the timing will be lost on the left-hand cylinder. Recheck the timing.

6 Provided that the contact breakers are in good condition and care is taken, manual adjustment of the ignition timing should be acceptably accurate. If possible, however, the timing should be checked using a stroboscopic lamp because not only can the accuracy of the timing be checked with the engine running but the correct performance of the ATU can be verified. The timing light should be connected to the low tension or high tension side of the ignition as instructed by the manufacturers of the light. Test the left-hand contact breaker and then the right-hand contact breaker. Start the engine and illuminate the ATU through the inspection aperture. With the engine running below 1500 rpm the F mark should be in alignment with the index mark. Raise the engine speed slowly to 3600 rpm when the advance mark should align with the index pointer. The advance mark on each side of the ATU takes the form of a scribed line to the right of the F mark. This line has no identification letter.

7 The advance range of 30° is between 1500 rpm, and 3600 rpm above which engine speed no more advance is possible. If, when increasing the engine speed from the commencement of advance, at 1500 rpm, the timing marks are seen to move erratically, or if the advance range has altered appreciably, the ATU should be inspected for wear or malfunctioning as described in the following Section.

8 Automatic timing unit: examination

1 The automatic timing unit rarely requires attention although it is advisable to examine it periodically.

2 To obtain access to the unit remove the inspection cover and the contact breaker back plate complete with contact breakers. The ATU centre bolt and engine turning hexagon should be removed before the stator plate. Before removal, the back plate should be marked so that it can be replaced in exactly the same position. This will ensure the ignition timing is not altered.

3 Pull the ATU from position, noting the drive pin with which it locates and is driven. The unit comprises balance weights which move outwards against spring tension as the centrifugal forces increase. The balance weights must move freely on their pivots which should be lubricated. The tension springs must also be in good condition.

4 Check the surface of the contact breaker cam for pitting or obvious signs of wear. Damage to the cam cannot be rectified; the complete ATU must be renewed.

5 When replacing the ATU, check that the drive pin engages with the recess in the rear of the centre boss. Because there is a single recess only, the ATU cannot be inadvertently replaced in the incorrect position and so alter the timing marks in relation to the crankshaft.

5.2 Remove centre screw and lead wire to free contact breaker

7.2a Timing marks on automatic timing unit (ATU)

7.2b ... can be seen easily through window in stator plate

7.4 A = LH cylinder timing adjustment screws, B = RH cylinder adjustment screws

9   Spark plugs: checking and resetting the gaps

1   All models are fitted with Nippon Denso type W24ES or NGK type B-8ES spark plugs as standard, gapped within the range 0·6 – 0·7 mm (0·024 – 0·028 in). Operating conditions may indicate a change in spark plug grade; the type recommended by the manufacturer gives the best, all round service.

2   Check the gap of the plug points during every three monthly or 3000 mile service. To reset the gap, bend the outer electrode to bring it closer to the centre electrode and check that a 0·6 mm (0·024 in) feeler gauge can be inserted. Never bend the central electrode or the insulator will crack, causing engine damage if the particles fall in whilst the engine is running.

3   With some experience, the condition of the spark plug electrodes and insulator can be used as a reliable guide to engine operating conditions. See accompanying illustrations.

4   Beware of overtightening the spark plugs, otherwise there is risk of stripping the threads from the aluminium alloy cylinder heads. The plugs should be sufficiently tight to sit firmly on their copper sealing washers, and no more. Use a spanner which is a good fit to prevent the spanner from slipping and breaking the insulator.

5   If the threads in the cylinder head strip as a result of overtightening the spark plugs, it is possible to reclaim the head by the use of a Helicoil thread insert. This is a cheap and convenient method of replacing the threads; most motorcycle dealers operate service of this kind.

6   Make sure the plug insulating caps are a good fit and have their rubber seals. They should also be kept clean to prevent tracking. These caps contain the suppressors that eliminate both radio and TV interference.

Spark plug maintenance: Checking plug gap with feeler gauges

Altering the plug gap. Note use of correct tool

Spark plug conditions: A brown, tan or grey firing end is indicative of correct engine running conditions and the selection of the appropriate heat rating plug

White deposits have accumulated from excessive amounts of oil in the combustion chamber or through the use of low quality oil. Remove deposits or a hot spot may form

Black sooty deposits indicate an over-rich fuel/air mixture, or a malfunctioning ignition system. If no improvement is obtained, try one grade hotter plug

Wet, oily carbon deposits form an electrical leakage path along the insulator nose, resulting in a misfire. The cause may be a badly worn engine or a malfunctioning ignition system

A blistered white insulator or melted electrode indicates over-advanced ignition timing or a malfunctioning cooling system. If correction does not prove effective, try a colder grade plug

A worn spark plug not only wastes fuel but also overloads the whole ignition system because the increased gap requires higher voltage to initiate the spark. This condition can also affect air pollution

8.4 Check cam for scoring and bob weights and springs for wear

10 Fault diagnosis: ignition system

Symptom	Cause	Remedy
Engine will not start	Faulty ignition switch	Operate switch several times in case contacts are dirty. If lights and other electrics function, switch may need renewal.
	Starter motor not working	Discharged battery. Use kickstart until battery is recharged.
	Short circuit in wiring	Check whether fuse is intact. Eliminate fault before switching on again.
	Completely discharged battery	If lights do not work, remove battery and recharge.
Engine misfires	Faulty condenser in ignition circuit	Renew condenser and re-test.
	Fouled spark plug	Renew plug and have original cleaned.
	Poor spark due to generator failure and discharge battery	Check output from generator. Remove and recharge battery.
Engine lacks power and overheats	Retarded ignition timing	Check timing and also contact breaker gap. Check whether auto-advance mechanism has jammed.
Engine 'fades' when under load	Pre-ignition	Check grade of plugs fitted: use recommended grades only.

Chapter 4 Frame and forks

Contents

Specifications

Front forks

Type	Hydraulically damped, telescopic
Damping fluid capacity	160 cc (5·4/4·5 US/Imp fl oz)
Damping fluid specification	50/50 mixture of SAE 10W/30 motor oil and ATF

Rear suspension

Type	Swinging arm supported on 5-position adjustable suspension units, pivoting on needle roller bearings

1 General description

The frame utilised on the GS400 models is of the duplex cradle type; that is, with the engine not comprising any part of the frame.

Rear suspension is of the swinging arm type, using oil filled suspension units to provide the necessary damping action. The units are adjustable so that the spring ratings can be varied within certain limits to match the load carried.

The front forks are of the conventional telescopic type, having internal, oil-filled dampers. The fork springs are contained within the fork stanchions and each fork leg can be detached from the machine as a complete unit, without dismantling the steering head assembly.

2 Front forks: removal from the frame

1 It is unlikely that the front forks will need to be removed from the frame as a complete unit, unless the steering head bearings require attention or the forks are damaged in an accident. In the event of damage to one or both of the fork legs, they may be removed from the steering head and lower fork yoke by following the procedure in this Section. If attention to the yokes and steering head bearings is required due to damage or wear, these components should be removed after fork leg removal by following the procedure given in the next Section.

2 Commence operations by placing the machine on the centre stand so that the front wheel is well clear of the ground. To raise the machine, the required amount of blocks should be placed below the crankcase. Remove the front wheel as described in Chapter 5, Section 3.

3 On disc brake machines, remove the two bolts which pass through the brake caliper, securing it to the fork leg. Swing the caliper unit back and suspend it from the frame by means of a length of wire or string. The hydraulic hose need not be disconnected from the caliper unit.

4 Detach the mudguard and remove it from between the fork legs. The mudguard is secured by two bolts passing into each fork leg.

5 Loosen the clamp bolts which retain the fork legs in the upper and lower yokes. The fork legs can now be eased downwards, out of position. If the clamps prove to be excessively tight, they may be gently sprung, using a large screwdriver. This must be done with great care, in order to prevent breakage of the clamps, necessitating renewal of the complete yoke.

6 The fork legs can now be dismantled for inspection and renovation as described in Section 4 of this Chapter.

2.4 Detach the mudguard held to each leg by two bolts

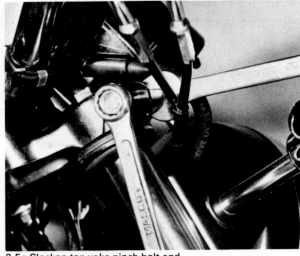

2.5a Slacken top yoke pinch bolt and ...

2.5b ... pinch bolt in the lower yoke

2.6 Withdraw fork leg downwards

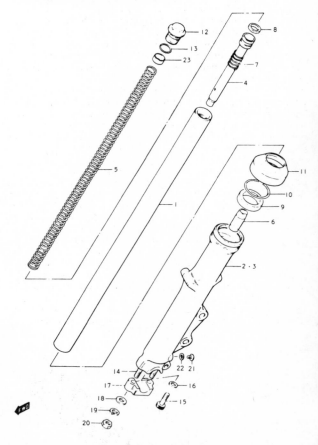

Fig. 4.1 Front forks

1 Stanchion – 2 off	13 'O' ring – 2 off
2 LH Lower leg	14 Stud – 4 off
3 RH Lower leg	15 Socket screw – 2 off
4 Damper rod – 2 off	16 Sealing washer – 2 off
5 Fork spring – 2 off	17 Wheel spindle clamp – 2 off
6 Damper rod seat – 2 off	18 Washer – 4 off
7 Rebound spring – 2 off	19 Spring washer – 4 off
8 Piston ring – 2 off	20 Nut – 4 off
9 Oil seal – 2 off	21 Drain plug – 2 off
10 Circlip – 2 off	22 Drain plug washer – 2 off
11 Dust excluder – 2 off	23 Spacer – 2 off
12 Domed bolt – 2 off	

3   Fork yoke and steering head: removal from the frame

1   Steering head and yoke removal should be commenced by removing the control cables from the handlebar levers or by removing the levers complete with cables. The shape of the handlebars fitted and the length of the control cables will probably dictate the method used.

2   On disc brake models only, remove the front brake lever master cylinder unit, which is retained by a clamp held by two bolts. Tie the master cylinder to some part of the machine not to be dismantled, so that it is secure and resting in an upright position.

3   Detach the handlebars from their mounting points on the fork upper yoke. The handlebars are held by two 'U' clamps, retained by two bolts and spring washers each. Remove the headlamp unit from the headlamp shell and disconnect the electrical leads at the snap connectors. No difficulty should be encountered in replacement, as the connections are mainly of the block type and the wiring is colour coded.

4   Disconnect the speedometer and tachometer cables at the instrument, where they are retained by knurled rings. Detach the wiring connections from the instrument bulb holders and from the warning lamp console (where fitted) at the two separate block connectors. Undo the two bolts which pass through the instrument mounting bracket and lift the complete unit from the machine.

5   Where a disc front brake is fitted remove the single bolt which secures the hydraulic hose union to the fork lower yoke. The complete front brake assembly, including the master cylinder, hoses and calipers, may be lifted away from the machine without the need to drain the fluid. By following this procedure, draining, refilling, and bleeding of the system is not required.

6   Loosen the clamp bolt located at the rear of the upper yoke, and from the top of the yoke remove the large chrome bolt together with the washer. From the underside tap the upper yoke upwards until it frees the steering column. Support the weight of the lower yoke and, using a 'C' spanner, remove the steering head bearing adjuster ring. If a 'C' spanner is not available a soft brass drift and hammer may be used to slacken the nut.

7   Remove the dust excluder and outer race (cone) once the adjuster nut has been detached. The bottom yoke, complete with steering column, can now be lowered from position. Make provision to catch the ball bearings as they are released; only the lower bearings will drop free since the upper bearings will most probably remain seated in the cup race retaining them.

4   Front forks: dismantling

1   It is advisable to dismantle each fork leg separately using an identical procedure. There is less chance of unwittingly exchanging parts if this approach is adopted. Commence by draining each fork leg of damping oil; there is a drain plug in each lower leg above and to the rear of each wheel spindle housing.

2   Remove the chromium plated bolt at the top of the fork leg and withdraw the spring upper seat and the fork spring. Some fork springs have variable pitch coils. Note carefully whether the coils are at the top or bottom of the fork on removal. The spring must be refitted in the same manner on subsequent reassembly.

3   Clamp the fork lower leg in a vice fitted with soft jaws, or wrap a length of rubber inner tube around the leg to prevent damage. Unscrew the socket screw, recessed into the housing which carries the front wheel spindle. Prise the dust excluder from position and slide it up the fork upper tube. The upper tube (stanchion) can be pulled out of the lower fork leg. Pull the damper rod seat off the rod, invert the upper tube and push the damper rod out of position towards the top end of the tube.

4   The oil seal fitted to the top of the lower leg should be removed only if it is to be renewed, because damage will almost certainly be inflicted when it is prised from position. The seal is retained by a spring clip.

4.2a Remove chromed top bolt and ...

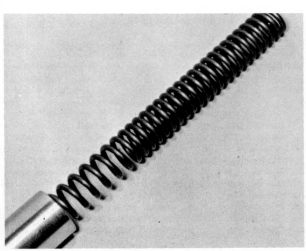

4.2b ... pull out fork spring from the leg

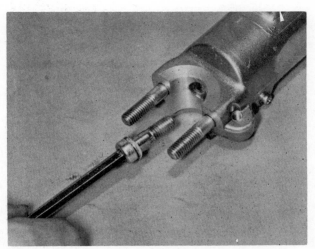

4.3a Remove socket screw from the lower leg

4.3b Prise off dust excluder and ...

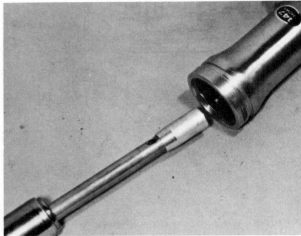

4.3c ... separate stanchion and damper rod from lower leg

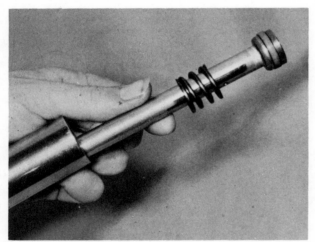

4.3d Invert stanchion to allow rod removal

4.4 The oil seal is retained by a spring clip

5   Front forks: examination and renovation

1   The front forks do not contain bushes. The fork legs slide directly against the outer hard chrome surface of the fork tubes. If wear occurs, indicated by slackness, the fork leg complete will have to be renewed, possibly also the fork stanchion. Wear of the fork stanchion is indicated by scuffing and penetration of the hard chrome surface.

2   Split or perished gaiters or dust covers must be attended to immediately otherwise the ingress of road grit will accelerate wear of the oil seal and upper tube.

3   After an extended period of service the fork springs may take a permanent set. If the spring lengths are suspect, they should be compared with a new set. It is wise to fit a new component if the overall length has decreased. Always fit new springs as a pair, NEVER separately.

4   Check the outer surface of the stanchion for scratches or roughness, it is only too easy to damage the oil seal during the re-assembly if these high spots are not eased down. The stanchions are unlikely to bend unless the machine is damaged in an accident. Any significant bend will be detected by eye, but if there is any doubt about straightness, roll the stanchion tubes on a flat surface. If the stanchions are bent, they must be renewed. Unless specialised repair equipment is available, it is rarely practicable to effect a satisfactory repair to a damaged stanchion.

5   The piston ring fitted to the damper rod may wear if oil changes at the specified intervals are neglected. If damping has become weakened and does not improve as a result of an oil change, the piston ring should be renewed. Check also that the oilways in the damper rod have not become obstructed.

6   Steering head bearings: examination and renovation

1   Clean and examine the cups and cones of the steering head bearings. They should have a polished appearance and show no signs of indentation. Renew the set if necessary.

2   Clean and examine the ball bearings which should also be polished and show no signs of surface cracks or blemishes. If any require replacement the whole set must be replaced.

3   Eighteen balls are fitted both in the top and bottom races. This arrangement will leave a gap but an extra ball must not be fitted otherwise the balls will press against each other, accentuating wear and making the steering stiff.

4   The outer races are a drive fit in the steering head lug and may be drifted out, using a suitable long handled drift passed through the centre of the lug. The lower inner race may be levered from position on the steering stem. When driving the new inner races into place, ensure that they remain square to the housing in the lug or the housing may be damaged.

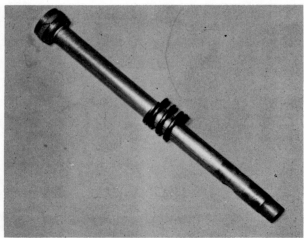

5.5 Renew damper ring if wear is evident

7 Front forks: replacement

1 Replace the front forks by following in reverse the dismantling procedure described in Sections 2 and 3 of this Chapter. Before fully tightening the front wheel spindle clamps and the fork yoke pinch bolts, bounce the forks several times to ensure they work correctly and settle down into their original settings.

2 Refill each fork leg with the correct quantity and specification of fork oil before replacing the handlebars. The handlebars obstruct access to the filler orifices. Fork oil capacity (per leg) is 160 cc (5·4/4·5 US/Imp fl oz).

Suzuki recommend that the damping fluid be a 50/50 mixture of fork oil or ATF and 10W/30 motor oil. Check that the drain plugs have been re-inserted and tightened before the oil is added.

3 If the fork stanchions prove difficult to relocate through the fork yokes, make sure their outer surfaces are clean and polished so that they will slide more easily. It is often advantageous to use a screwdriver blade to open up the clamps, as the tubes are moved upwards into position.

4 Before the machine is used on the road, check the adjustment of the steering head bearings. If they are too slack, judder

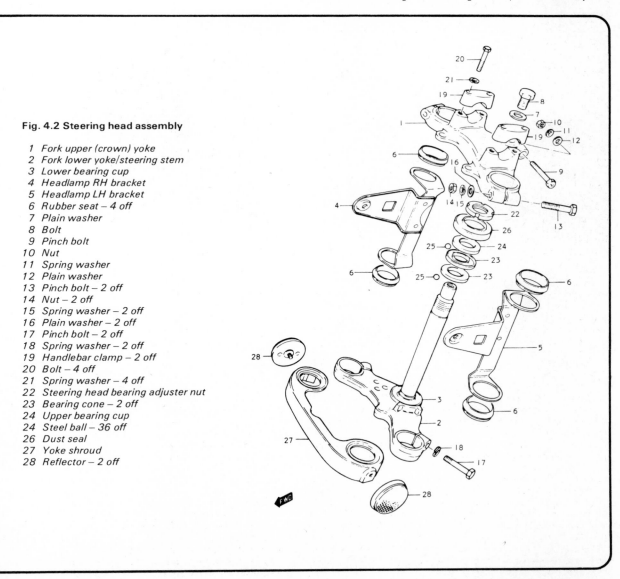

Fig. 4.2 Steering head assembly

 1 Fork upper (crown) yoke
 2 Fork lower yoke/steering stem
 3 Lower bearing cup
 4 Headlamp RH bracket
 5 Headlamp LH bracket
 6 Rubber seat – 4 off
 7 Plain washer
 8 Bolt
 9 Pinch bolt
10 Nut
11 Spring washer
12 Plain washer
13 Pinch bolt – 2 off
14 Nut – 2 off
15 Spring washer – 2 off
16 Plain washer – 2 off
17 Pinch bolt – 2 off
18 Spring washer – 2 off
19 Handlebar clamp – 2 off
20 Bolt – 4 off
21 Spring washer – 4 off
22 Steering head bearing adjuster nut
23 Bearing cone – 2 off
24 Upper bearing cup
24 Steel ball – 36 off
26 Dust seal
27 Yoke shroud
28 Reflector – 2 off

will occur, especially during braking. There should be no detectable play in the head races when the handlebars are pulled and pushed with the front brake applied hard.

5   Overtight head races are equally undesirable. It is possible to unwittingly apply a loading of several tons on the head races when they have been overtightened, even though the handlebars appear to turn quite freely. Overtight bearings will make the machine roll at low speeds and give generally imprecise handling with a tendency to weave. Adjustment is correct if there is no perceptible play in the bearings and the handlebars will swing to full lock in either direction, when the machine is on the centre stand with the front wheel clear of the ground. Only a slight tap should cause the handlebars to swing.

8   Steering head lock

1   A steering head lock is attached to the underside of the lower yoke of the forks by two screws and washers. When in a locked position, a tongue extends from the body of the lock when the handlebars are on full lock in either direction and abuts against a plate welded to the base of the steering head. In consequence, the handlebars cannot be turned until the lock is released.

2   If the lock malfunctions, it must be renewed. A repair is impracticable. When the lock is changed the key must be changed too, to match the new lock.

9   Frame: examination and renovation

1   The frame is unlikely to require attention unless accident damage has occurred. In some cases, replacement of the frame is the only satisfactory course of action if it is badly out of alignment. Only a few frame repair specialists have the jigs and mandrels necessary for resetting the frame to the required standard of accuracy and even then there is no easy means of assessing to what extent the frame may have been overstressed.

2   After the machine has covered a considerable mileage, it is advisable to examine the frame closely for signs of cracking or splitting at the welded joints. Rust can also cause weakness at these joints. Minor damage can be repaired by welding or brazing, depending on the extent and nature of the damage.

3   Remember that a frame which is out of alignment will cause handling problems and may even promote 'speed wobbles'. If misalignment is suspected, as the result of an accident, it will be necessary to strip the machine completely so that the frame can be checked and, if necessary, renewed.

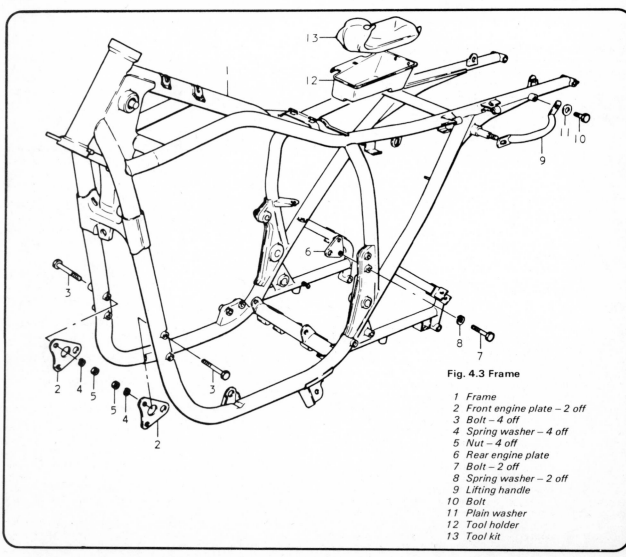

Fig. 4.3 Frame

1 Frame
2 Front engine plate – 2 off
3 Bolt – 4 off
4 Spring washer – 4 off
5 Nut – 4 off
6 Rear engine plate
7 Bolt – 2 off
8 Spring washer – 2 off
9 Lifting handle
10 Bolt
11 Plain washer
12 Tool holder
13 Tool kit

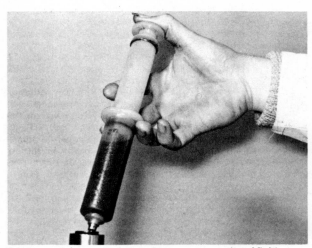
7.2 Do not forget to fill forks with correct quantity of fluid

8.1 Steering lock is screwed to underside of fork lower yoke

10 Swinging arm fork: dismantling and renovation

1   The rear fork of the frame is of the swinging arm type. It pivots on a shaft that passes through the crossmember and both sides of the main frame assembly, with a spacing collar, two inner bushes, and two needle roller bearings. The whole assembly is held together with a pivot shaft that is bolted up with a nut at one end.
    Worn swinging arm bushes can be detected by placing the machine on its centre stand and pulling and pushing vigorously on the rear wheel in a horizontal direction. Any play will be magnified by the leverage effect.
2   When wear develops in the swinging arm, necessitating renewal of the bearings, the renovation procedure is quite straightforward. Commence by removing the rear wheel as described in Chapter 5, Section 10.
3   The final drive chainguard is secured by three bolts. Removal is not strictly necessary, although it will facilitate swinging arm detachment.
4   Remove the lower two nuts that hold the suspension units to the swinging fork, so that the fork swings down. Leave the suspension units hanging from the frame, but slacken the top nut so that they are free to move. This facilitates reassembly.
5   Take out the swinging arm pivot shaft undoing the nut on the left-hand side of the machine. The spindle may need a gently tap with a rawhide mallet and drift to displace it. Pull the final drive chain across so that it clears the swinging arm fork left-hand end. The swinging arm is now free and can be lifted out to the rear.
6   Remove the dust cap and thrust washer from each side of the swinging arm cross-member and then pull out the two short bushes. Push out the long central spacer, using a long shanked screwdriver. A circlip fitted to the spacer on original assembly will be displaced as the spacer is removed. The circlip served a useful purpose only during factory assembly and therefore may be discarded.
7   The caged needle roller bearings may be drifted out of position, using a suitable length of steel rod. Do not remove the bearings merely for inspection as the cages will be damaged by the drift. Lubricate the outside of the new bearing cages before driving them into place, and ensure that they are fitted with the punch marked face outwards.
8   Check that the swinging arm pivot shaft is straight. A bent shaft may be straightened in a jig. If this cannot be

accomplished, the shaft should be renewed.
9   Reassemble the swinging arm fork by reversing the dismantling procedure. Grease the pivot shaft and bearings liberally prior to reassembly. After reassembly, additional lubrication should be carried out via the grease nipple fitted to the upper side of the swinging arm cross member.

11 Rear suspension units: examination

1   Rear suspension units of the hydraulically damped type are fitted to the Suzuki GS models. They can be adjusted to give five different spring loadings, without removal from the machine.
2   Each rear suspension unit has two peg holes immediately above the adjusting notches, to facilitate adjustment. Either a 'C' spanner or the screwdriver supplied with the original tool kit can be used to turn the adjusters. Turn clockwise to increase the spring tension and stiffen up the rear suspension.
    The recommended settings are:-
    Position 1 (least tension) for normal solo riding and
    Position 5 (greatest tension) for both high speed riding or when carrying a heavy load. The intermediate settings may be used for varying conditions, as required.
3   The suspension units are sealed and there is no means of topping up or changing the damping fluid. If the damping fails or if the unit leaks, renewal is necessary.
4   In the interests of good roadholding it is essential that both suspension units have the same load setting. If renewal is necessary, the units must be replaced as a matched pair.

12 Centre stand: examination

1   The centre stand is retained to the underside of the frame by two bolts which serve as pivot shafts. A bush is fitted to each shaft. The pivot assembly on centre stands are often neglected with regard to lubrication and this will eventually lead to wear. It is prudent to remove the pivot bushes from time to time and grease them thoroughly. This will prolong the effective life of the stand.
2   Check that the return spring is in good condition. A broken or weak spring may cause the stand to fall whilst the machine is being ridden, and catch in some obstacle, unseating the rider.

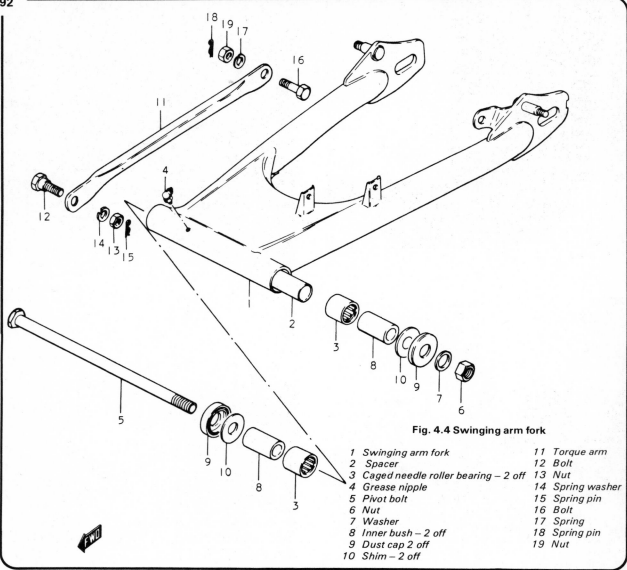

Fig. 4.4 Swinging arm fork

1	Swinging arm fork	11	Torque arm
2	Spacer	12	Bolt
3	Caged needle roller bearing – 2 off	13	Nut
4	Grease nipple	14	Spring washer
5	Pivot bolt	15	Spring pin
6	Nut	16	Bolt
7	Washer	17	Spring
8	Inner bush – 2 off	18	Spring pin
9	Dust cap 2 off	19	Nut
10	Shim – 2 off		

10.3 Final drive chain guard is held by three bolts

10.4 Detach suspension units at lower mounting points

10.5a Remove nut and withdraw spindle to allow . . .

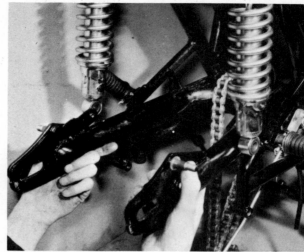

10.5b . . . swinging arm removal towards the rear

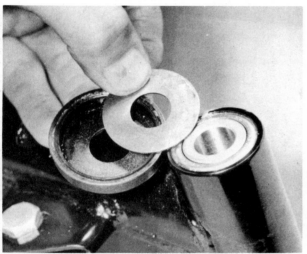

10.6a Note thrust washers below dust caps

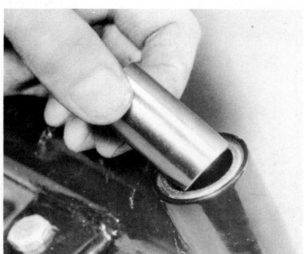

10.6b Pull out inner (short) bushes followed by . . .

10.6c . . . long central bush

10.7 Bearing may be driven out with long shanked punch

13 Prop stand: examination

1   The prop stand bolts to a lug attached to the rear of the left-hand lower frame tube. An extension spring ensures that the stand is retracted when the weight of the machine is taken off the stand.

2   Check that the pivot bolt is secure and that the extension spring is in good condition and not over-stretched. An accident is almost inevitable if the stand extends whilst the machine is on the move.

14 Footrests: examination and renovation

1   The front footrests on all models are of the bolt-on type, with fixed rubber pads. If they are bent in a spill or through the machine falling over, they can be removed and straightened in a vice whilst heated to a dull red with a blow lamp, or welding torch. The pillion footrests are hinged and therefore are less likely to become damaged than the front footrests. Each peg pivots on a clevis pin secured by a washer and split pin.

15 Brake pedal: examination

1   The rear brake pedal is secured by a single pinch bolt to the splined brake pivot shaft. In the event of damage, the pedal may be removed and treated similarly to a bent footrest as described in the previous Section.

2   The pedal may be pulled off the shaft after removing completely the pinch bolt. The outer end of the brake return spring, which shares the pivot shaft, should be displaced from the anchor peg on the frame, so that it may be removed at the same time as the pedal.

16 Dualseat: removal and replacement

1   The dualseat is attached to two lugs on the left side of the frame by two clevis pins secured with split pins. If it is necessary to remove the dualseat, withdraw the two split pins, take out the clevis pins, and the seat will lift off as a complete unit.

17 Speedometer and tachometer heads: removal and replacement

1   The speedometer and tachometer are mounted together on a single panel on top of the front forks. They are secured in position by nuts on two studs projecting from the base of each instrument and passing through the shared mounting bracket and the base cover.

2   The instruments may be detached from the machine as a unit, after disconnecting the drive cables and the warning bulb leads at the block connector. After removing the base plate, the bulb holders may be pulled from position.

3   If either instrument fails to record, check the drive cable first before suspecting the head. If the instrument gives a jerky response it is probably due to a dry cable, or one that is trapped or kinked.

4   The speedometer and tachometer heads cannot be repaired by the private owner, and if a defect occurs a new instrument has to be fitted. Remember that a speedometer in correct working order is required by law on a machine in the UK and also in many other countries.

5   Speedometer and tachometer cables are supplied only as a complete assembly. Make sure the cables are routed correctly through the clamps provided on the top fork yoke and the frame.

18 Speedometer and tachometer drives: location and examination

1   In the case of the disc front brake machines, the speedometer drive gearbox is fitted on the left-hand side of the front wheel hub. On drum front brake machines the gearbox is an integral part of the brake plate and is driven internally from the front hub. In both cases the drive rarely gives trouble provided it is kept properly lubricated. Lubrication should take place whenever the front wheel is removed for wheel bearing inspection or replacement.

2   The tachometer drive is taken from the cylinder head cover, between the two cylinders. The drive is taken from the overhead exhaust camshaft by means of skew-cut pinions and then by a flexible cable to the tachometer head. It is unlikely that the internal drive will give trouble during the normal service life of the machine, particularly since it is fully enclosed and effectively lubricated.

19 Cleaning the machine

1   After removing all surface dirt with a rag or sponge which is washed frequently in clean water, the machine should be allowed to dry thoroughly. Application of car polish or wax to the cycle parts will give a good finish, particularly if the machine receives this attention at regular intervals.

2   The plated parts should require only a wipe with a damp rag, but if they are badly corroded, as may occur during the winter when the roads are salted, it is permissible to use one of the proprietary chrome cleaners. These often have an oily base which will help to prevent corrosion from recurring.

3   If the engine parts are particularly oily, use a cleaning compound such as Gunk or Jizer. Apply the compound whilst the parts are dry and work it in with a brush so that it has an opportunity to penetrate and soak into the film of oil and grease. Finish off by washing down liberally, taking care that water does not enter the carburettors, air cleaners or the electrics. If desired, the now clean aluminium alloy parts can be enhanced still further when they are dry by using a special polish such as Solvol Autosol. This will restore the full lustre.

4   If possible, the machine should be wiped down immediately after it has been used in the wet, so that it is not garaged under damp conditions which will promote rusting. Make sure that the chain is wiped and re-oiled, to prevent water from entering the rollers and causing harshness with an accompanying rapid rate of wear. Remember there is less chance of water entering the control cables and causing stiffness if they are lubricated regularly as described in the Routine Maintenance Section.

20 Fault diagnosis: frame and forks

Symptom	Cause	Remedy
Machine is unduly sensitive to road conditions	Forks and/or rear suspension units have defective damping	Check oil level in front forks. Renew rear suspension units.
Machine tends to roll at low speeds	Steering head bearings overtight or damaged	Slacken bearing adjustment. If no improvement, dismantle and inspect bearings.
Machine tends to wander, steering is imprecise	Worn swinging arm bearings	Check and if necessary renew bearings.
Fork action stiff	Fork legs have twisted in yokes or have been drawn together at lower ends	Slacken off spindle nut clamps, pinch bolts in fork yokes and bounce forks several times before retightening from bottom.
Forks judder when front brake is aplied	Worn fork legs and stanchions Steering head bearings too slack	Renew one or both items. Readjust to take up play.
Wheels out of alignment	Frame distorted as result of accident damage	Check frame alignment after stripping out. If bent, specialist repair is necessary.

Chapter 5 Wheels, brakes and tyres

Contents

Specifications

Tyres
Front . . . . 3·00 S 18 in
Rear . . . . 3·50 S 18 in

Tyre pressures

	Solo	Pillion
Front	25 psi	25 psi
Rear	28 psi	32 psi

1 General description

The GS400 model is fitted with 18 inch wheels at both the front and rear. The front tyre has a section of 3·00 inches, and the rear tyre one of 3·50 inches. The wheels are of traditional design having a steel rim laced to an aluminium alloy hub by chromed spokes.

The GS400B and 400C are fitted with a single disc brake on the front wheel, the GS400XB has a twin leading shoe brake of traditional design. Both models utilise the same single leading shoe rear brake.

2 Front wheel: examination and renovation

1   Place the machine on the centre sat the front wheel is raised clear of the ground. Spin the wheel and check the rim alignment. Small irregularities can be corrected by tightening the spokes in the affected area although a certain amount of experience is necessary to prevent over-correction. Any flats in the wheel rim will be evident at the same time. These are more difficult to remove and in most cases it will be necessary to have the wheel rebuilt on a new rim. Apart from the effect on stability, a flat will expose the tyre bead and walls to greater risk of damage if the machine is run with a deformed wheel.

2   Check for loose and broken spokes. Tapping the spokes is the best guide to tension. A loose spoke will produce a quite different sound and should be tightened by turning the nipple in an anticlockwise direction. Always check for run out by spinning the wheel again. If the spokes have to be tightened by an excessive amount, it is advisable to remove the tyre and tube as detailed in Section 19 of this Chapter. This will enable the protruding ends of the spokes to be ground off, thus preventing them from chafing the inner tube and causing punctures.

3 Front wheel: removal and replacement

1   Place the machine on the centre stand so that it is resting securely on firm ground with the front wheel well clear of the ground. If necessary, place wooden blocks below the crankcase to raise the wheel.

2   On drum brake models remove the split pin from the lower end of the front brake cable and undo the adjuster nut. Withdraw the cable from the brake actuating arm and displace the trunnion. Refit all components onto the cable to avoid loss.

3   Disconnect the speedometer at the gearbox by unscrewing the knurled ring. Pull the cable through the guide clip. Displace the split pin from the wheel spindle nut and slacken the nut slightly. The wheel may be removed either by detaching the two spindle clamps or by slackening the clamp bolts and withdrawing the spindle. Note the positioning of the wheel spacers, and on disc brake models, the speedometer gearbox.

4   When refitting the wheel into the forks on disc brake models, ensure that the speedometer gearbox is fitted with the embossed arrow-mark pointing upwards. On drum brake models, make certain that the recess in the brake plate engages correctly with the lug projecting from the fork left-hand leg. If this does not align correctly, there is nothing to restrain the brake plate and it will revolve when the brake is applied, causing a serious accident.

5   Tighten the wheel spindle nut fully before tightening the two spindle clamps, and do not omit the split pin. The two nuts holding each spindle clamp should be tightened down evenly so that the gap between the clamp and fork leg is equal either side of the wheel spindle.

3.3a Unscrew speedometer drive cable

3.3b Remove split pin and nut and ...

3.3c ... slacken clamps to allow spindle removal

3.4a Dogs on gearbox must engage with slots in hub

3.4b Position arrow upwards when wheel is fitted

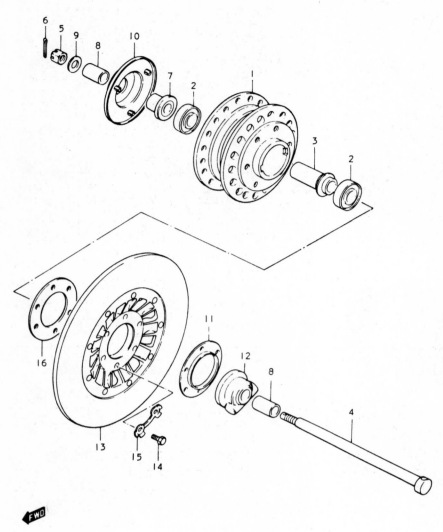

Fig. 5.1 Front hub – Disc brake models

 1 *Hub*
 2 *Bearing – 2 off*
 3 *Bearing spacer*
 4 *Front wheel spindle*
 5 *Castellated nut*
 6 *Split pin*
 7 *Spacer*
 8 *Spacer – 2 off*
 9 *Washer*
10 *RH cover*
11 *LH cover*
12   *Speedometer gearbox*
13 *Brake disc*
14 *Bolt – 6 off*
15 *Locking plate – 3 off*
16 *Backing plate*

4   Front disc brake assembly: examination and brake pad renewal

1   Check the front brake master cylinder, hoses and caliper unit for signs of leakage. Pay particular attention to the condition of the hoses, which should be renewed without question if there are signs of cracking, splitting or other exterior damage. Check the hydraulic fluid level by referring to the upper and lower level lines visible on the exterior of the translucent reservoir body.

2   Replenish the reservoir after removing the cap on the brake fluid reservoir and lifting out the diaphragm plate. The condition of the fluid is one of the maintenance tasks which should **never be neglected**. If the fluid is below the lower level mark, brake fluid of the correct specification must be added. **Never** use engine oil or any fluid other than that recommended. Other fluids have unsatisfactory characteristics and will rapidly destroy the seals.

3   The two sets of brake pads should be inspected for wear. Each has a red groove, which marks the wear limit of the friction material. When this limit is reached, both pads in the set must be renewed, even if only one has reached the wear mark.

4   If the brake action becomes spongy, or if any part of the hydraulic system is dismantled (such as when a hose has been renewed) it is necessary to bleed the system in order to remove all traces of air. Follow the procedure in Section 6 of this Chapter.

5   To gain access to the pads for renewal, the caliper assembly may be detached from the front fork, in which case the front wheel need not be removed. If the wheel is already removed, detachment of the caliper is not required. In the former case disconnection of the hydraulic hose is not required.

6   Remove the single screw and the convolute backing plate from the inner side of the caliper unit. The inner pad is now free and may be displaced towards the centre of the caliper and lifted out. The outer pad which abuts against the caliper piston is not retained positively and may be lifted out.

7   Refit the new pads and replace the caliper by reversing the dismantling procedure. The caliper piston should be pushed inwards slightly so that there is sufficient clearance between the brake pads to allow the caliper to fit over the disc. It is recommended that the outer periphery of the outer (piston) pad is lightly coated with disc brake assembly grease (silicon grease). Use the grease sparingly and ensure that grease **DOES NOT** come in contact with the friction surface of the pad.

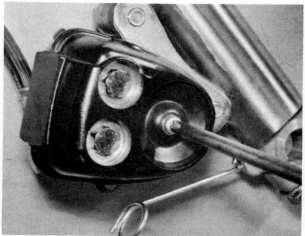

4.6a Unscrew centrescrew and remove plate to free ...

4.6b ... inner pad

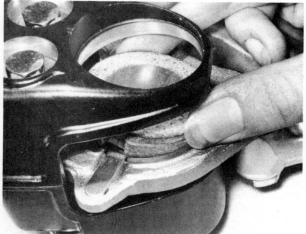

4.6c Outer pad is a free push fit

4.6d Pads have wear limit grooves to aid examination

5 Front brake caliper: examination and overhaul

1   Select a suitable receptacle into which may be drained the hydraulic fluid. Remove the banjo bolt holding the hydraulic hose at the caliper and allow the fluid to drain. Take great care not to allow hydraulic fluid to spill onto paintwork; it is a very effective paint stripper. Hydraulic fluid will also damage rubber and plastic components.

2   Remove the caliper from the fork leg and displace the brake pads as described in the preceding Section.

3   Remove the two bolts which pass through the caliper body, and separate the body from the caliper support bracket. Prise out the piston boot, using a small screwdriver, taking care not to scratch the surface of the cylinder bore. The piston can be displaced most easily by applying an air jet to the hydraulic fluid feed orifice. Be prepared to catch the piston as it falls free. Displace the annular piston seal from the cylinder bore groove.

4   Clean the caliper components thoroughly in trichlorethylene or in hydraulic brake fluid. CAUTION: Never use petrol for cleaning hydraulic brake parts otherwise the rubber components will be damaged. Discard all the rubber components as a matter of

course. The replacement cost is relatively small and does not warrant re-use of components vital to safety. Check the piston and caliper cylinder bore for scoring, rusting or pitting. If any of these defects are evident it is unlikely that a good fluid seal can be maintained and for this reason the components should be renewed.

5   To assemble the caliper, reverse the removal procedure. When assembling pay attention to the following points. Apply Suzuki caliper grease (high heat resistance) to the caliper spindles. Apply a generous amount of brake fluid to the inner surface of the cylinder and to the periphery of the piston, then reassemble. Do not reassemble the piston with it inclined or twisted. When installing the piston push it slowly into the cylinder while taking care not to damage the piston seal. Apply Suzuki brake pad grease around the periphery of the moving pad. Bleed the brake after refilling the reservoir with new hydraulic brake fluid, then check for leakage while applying the brake lever tightly. After a test run, check the pads and brake disc.

6   Note that any work on the hydraulic system must be undertaken under ultra-clean conditions. Particles of dirt will score the working parts and cause early failure.

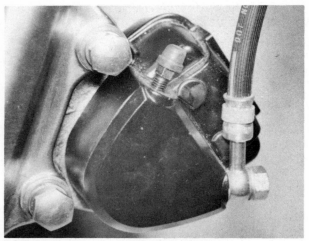

5.2 Caliper is secured to fork leg by two bolts

5.3 Remove these two bolts to separate caliper from support

5.5 Support must be free to slide on spindle bolts

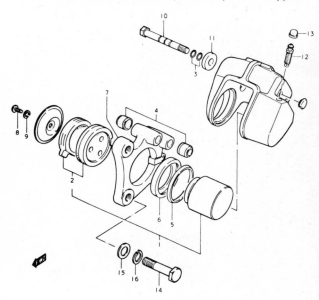

Fig. 5.2 Front brake caliper

6 Front disc brake master cylinder: examination and renovation

1   The master cylinder and hydraulic reservoir take the form of a combined unit mounted on the right-hand side of the handlebars, to which the front brake lever is attached. The master cylinder is actuated by the front brake lever, and applies hydraulic pressure through the system to operate the front brake when the handlebar lever is manipulated. The master cylinder pressurises the hydraulic fluid in the brake pipe which, being incompressible, causes the piston to move in the caliper unit and apply the friction pads to the brake disc. If the master cylinder seals leak, hydraulic pressure will be lost and the braking action rendered much less effective.

2   Before the master cylinder can be removed, the system must be drained. Place a clean container below the caliper unit and attach a plastic tube from the bleed screw on top of the caliper unit to the container. Open the bleed screw one complete turn and drain the system by operating the brake lever until the master cylinder reservoir is empty. Close the bleed screw and remove the pipe.

3   Remove the front brake stop lamp switch from the master cylinder (where fitted). Unscrew the union bolt and disconnect the connection between the brake hose and the master cylinder.

1 Piston/pad set	9 Spring washer
2 Pad set	10 Spindle bolt – 2 off
3 'O' ring – 4 off	11 Washer – 2 off
4 Dust cover – 4 off	12 Bleed nipple
5 Piston seal	13 Dust cap
6 Piston boot	14 Bolt – 2 off
7 Caliper support bracket	15 Plain washer – 2 off
8 Screw	16 Spring washer – 2 off

Unscrew the two master cylinder fastening bolts and remove the master cylinder body from the handlebar. Empty any surplus fluid from the reservoir.

4   Remove the brake lever from the body, remove the boot stopper (taking care not to damage the boot) and then remove the boot. Remove the circlip that was hidden by the boot, the piston, primary cup, spring and check valve. Place the parts in a clean container and wash them in new brake fluid. Examine the cylinder bore and piston for scoring. Renew if scored. Check also the brake lever for pivot wear, cracks or fractures, the hose union threads and brake pipe threads for cracks or other signs of deterioration.

5 When assembling the master cylinder follow the removal procedure in reverse order. Pay particular attention to the following points: Make sure the primary cup is fitted the correct way round. Renew the split pin of the brake lever pivot nut and fit it securely. Mount the master cylinder on the handlebars so the gap between it and the switch is 2 mm (0·08 in), and the reservoir is horizontal when the motorcycle is on the centre stand with the steering in the straight ahead direction. Fill with fresh fluid and bleed the system. Be sure to check the brake reservoir by removing the reservoir cap. If the level is below the ring mark inside the reservoir, refill to the level with the pre-scribed brake fluid.

6 The component parts of the master cylinder assembly and the caliper assembly may wear or deteriorate in function over a long period of use. It is however, generally difficult to foresee how long each component will work with proper efficiency. From a safety point of view it is best to change all the expend-able parts every two years on a machine that has covered a normal mileage.

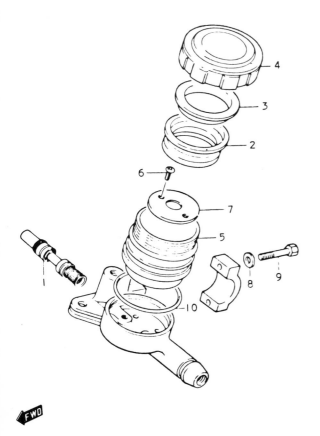

Fig. 5.3 Master cylinder

    1 Piston cup assembly
    2 Diaphragm
    3 Diaphragm plate
    4 Reservoir cap
    5 Reservoir
    6 Screw – 2 off
    7 Plate
    8 Washer – 2 off
    9 Bolt – 2 off
    10 'O'ring

7 Bleeding the hydraulic brake system

1 If the hydraulic system has to be drained and refilled, if the front brake lever travel becomes excessive or the lever operates with a soft or spongy feeling, the brakes must be bled to expel air from the system. The procedure for bleeding the hydraulic brake is best carried out by two persons.

2 First check the fluid level in the reservoir and top up with fresh fluid.

3 Keep the reservoir at least half full of fluid during the bleed-ing procedure.

4 Screw the cap on to the reservoir to prevent a spout of fluid or the entry of dust into the system. Place a clean glass jar below the caliper bleed screw and attach a clear plastic pipe from the caliper bleed screw to the container. Place some clean hydraulic fluid in the jar so that the pipe is always immersed below the surface of the fluid.

5 Unscrew the bleed screw one half turn and squeeze the brake lever as far as it will go but do not release it until the bleeder valve is closed again. Repeat the operation a few times until no more air bubbles come from the plastic tube.

6 Keep topping up the reservoir with new fluid. When all the bubbles disappear, close the bleeder valve dust cap. Check the fluid level in the reservoir, after the bleeding operation has been completed.

7 Reinstall the diaphragm and tighten the reservoir cap securely. Do not use the brake fluid drained from the system, since it will contain minute air bubbles.

8 Never use any fluid other than that recommended. Oil must not be used under any circumstances.

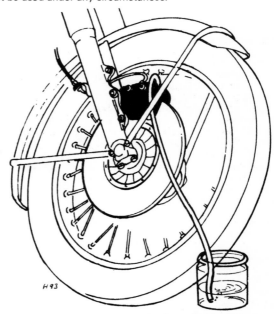

Fig. 5.4 Bleeding the front disc brake

8 Removing and replacing the disc

1 It is unlikely that the brake disc will require attention unless bad scoring has developed or the disc have warped. To detach the disc first remove the wheel as described in Section 3 of this Chapter. The disc is retained by six bolts screwed into the hub, which are linked in pairs by tab washers. Bend down the ears of the tab washers and remove the bolts. The disc can then be eased off the hub bosses.

2 Replace the disc by reversing the dismantling procedure. Ensure that the six bolts are tightened fully and that the tab washer ears are bent up against the bolt head flats.

8.2 Always secure disc bolts with locking tabs on reassembly

9.4 Lift shoes into 'V' form for easy removal

9   Front wheel drum brake: examination and renovation

1   After removal of the front wheel the brake plate complete with brake shoes and speedometer gear can be removed from the wheel hub.

2   Examine the brake linings for oil, dirt or grease. Surface dirt can be removed with a stiff brush but oil soaked linings should be renewed. High spots can be carefully eased down with emery cloth.

3   Examine the condition of the brake linings and if they have worn thin they should be renewed. The brake linings are bonded to the brake shoes and thus separate linings are not available.

4   To remove the shoes, pull them away from the two cams and from the plate in a 'V' formation so that they can be removed together, complete with the return springs. When they are well clear of the brake plate the springs can be removed. Check the springs for any signs of wear or stretching and renew if necessary. Check the surface of the brake drum for wear or scoring.

5   Whilst the brake plate is off, the brake cam spindle should be lubricated sparingly with grease. Before removing the linkage between the cams, check that both the cams and the levers are marked (usually centre punched) so that they can be replaced in the same positions. Mark them clearly, if they are not so marked. Slacken both pinch bolts and then draw off the linkage assembly complete. It will probably be tight and will have to be levered off gently with a screwdriver, being careful not to damage the alloy brake plate. Do not undo the connecting brake rod locknut otherwise realignment will be required on reassembly.

6   Brush all the dust from the brake plate and reassemble in the reverse order to the above. Do not forget the 'O' rings on the cam spindle and to lightly grease the cams, spindles and the fixed spindle at the other end of the brake shoe.

7   The speedometer drive located in the brake plate should not require attention except for cleaning and new grease. Examine the oil seal and obtain a replacement, if required.

8   Dust out the brake drum and examine it for score marks and damage. It should have a shiny, smooth surface. Clean the drum with a petrol soaked rag to remove all traces of grease.

9   When reassembling the wheel and brake do not get any grease or oil on the brake shoes or drum.

10   Adjusting the front brake (twin leading shoe drum brake only)

1   In order for the twin leading shoe front brake to operate at full efficiency the leading edges of the brake linings must come into contact with the brake drum at exactly the same time when the brake is applied. It is also important that an equal amount of leverage is applied to the two brake operating cams. This is effected by ensuring that the two brake arms are set parallel to each other. If the arms are not parallel to each other, the effective length of the rearmost operating lever is reduced, thereby lowering the leverage ratio of the operating cam.

2   If, during front brake maintenance the relative positions of the two operating levers were not punch marked to ensure easy and accurate reassembly the brake can be reset with the wheel in place in the forks as follows:

Place the main (long) brake operating arm on the splines of the front operating cam so that when the operating cable is attached to the arm and the arm is pulled into the 'ON' position, the angle between the arm and the cable is slightly less than 90°. If the angle is found to be more than 90° pull the arm off the splines and refit it in the next position in a clockwise direction.

3   Fit the brake operating cable, and whilst spinning the front wheel, adjust the nut on the cable end until the brake just begins to bite. Slacken off the nut $\frac{1}{2}$ a turn. Loosen the locknut on the cam arm connecting rod and fit the rear brake arm onto the camshaft splines so that the two arms are parallel. Spin the wheel again and turn the adjusting rod until the rear arm moves sufficiently to make the brake just bite. Slacken the adjuster rod half a turn. The two operating arms should now to all intents and purposes be parallel. Tighten the locknut on the connecting rod and tighten the two brake arm pinch bolts.

4   Adjust the operating cable at the handlebar lever so that there is approximately 25 mm (1 in) movement at the lever end before braking action commences.

11   Front wheel bearings: examination and replacement

All models

1   Place the machine on the centre stand and remove the front wheel as described in Section 3. On disc brake machines remove the speedometer gearbox from the left-hand side of the hub, prise off the plastic cover and remove the spacer from the

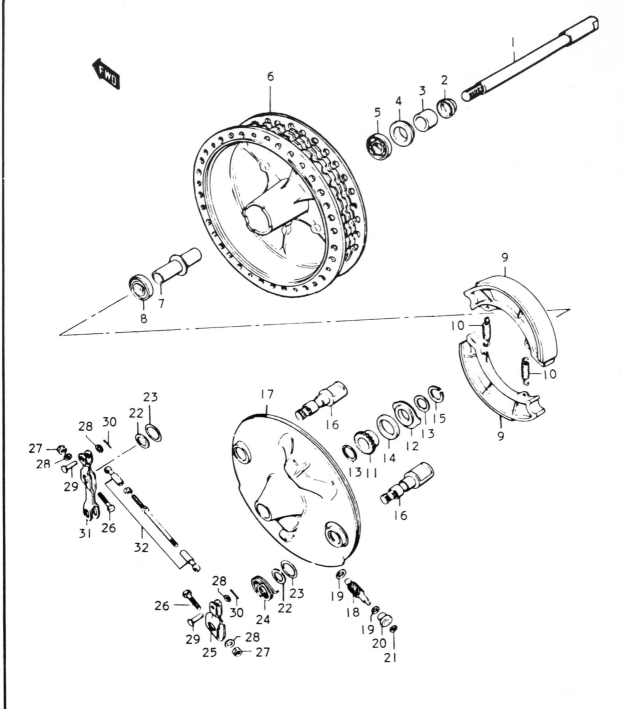

Fig. 5.5 Front hub assembly – drum brake models

1 Front wheel spindle	10 Return spring – 2 off	18 Speedometer worm shaft
2 Dust cover	11 Speedometer gear	19 Thrust washer – 2 off
3 Spacer	12 Drive dog	20 Bush
4 Oil seal	13 Washer – 2 off	21 Oil seal
5 Wheel bearing	14 Oil seal	22 Washer – 2 off
6 Front hub	15 Circlip	23 'O'ring – 2 off
7 Bearing spacer	16 Brake operating cam – 2 off	24 Spring
8 Bearing	17 Brake back plate	25 Secondary brake operating
9 Brake shoe – 2 off		

lever
26 Bolt – 2 off
27 Nut – 2
28 Washer – 4 off
29 Clevis pin – 2 off
30 Split pin – 2 off
31 Primary brake operating lever
32 Link rod

right-hand side of the hub. To gain access to the bearings on drum brake machines, first remove the brake plate on the left-hand side of the hub and the dust excluder and spacer from the right-hand side of the hub.

2   The wheel bearings can now be tapped out from each side with the use of a suitable long drift. Careful and even tapping will prevent the bearing 'tying' and damage to the races. It may be necessary to tap the wheel bearing spacer to one side to expose the edge of the inner race and enable the drift to be used. On drum brake models the oil seal fitted to the hub will be driven out by the bearing.

3   Remove all the old grease from the hub and bearings, giving the latter a final wash in petrol. When the bearings are clean, lubricate them sparingly with a very light oil. Check the bearings for play and roughness when they are spun by hand. All used bearings will emit a small amount of noise when spun but they should not chatter or sound rough. If there is any doubt about the conditions of the bearings they should be renewed.

4   Before replacing the bearings pack them with high melting point grease. Do not overfill the hub centre with grease as it will expand when hot and may find its way past the oil seals. The hub space should be about $\frac{2}{3}$ full of grease. Drift the bearings in, using a soft drift on the outside ring of the bearing. Do not drift the centre ring of the bearing or damage will be incurred. Replace the oil seal carefully, drifting it into place with a thick walled tube of approximately the same dimensions as the oil seal. A large socket spanner is ideal. Bearings using integral seals must be fitted with the sealed side outermost.

12 Rear wheel: examination , removal and renovation

1   Place the machine on the centre stand so that the rear wheel is raised clear of the ground. Check for rim alignment, damage to the rim and loose or broken spokes by following the procedure relating to the front wheel, as described in Section 2 of this Chapter.

2   Before removing the wheel it is recommended that both silencers are detached to improve access. On 400C models the exhaust pipes should be detached also. Each is retained by two bolts passing through two separate brackets welded to the silencer body. The silencer/exhaust pipe clamps should be slackened before drawing the silencers off.

3   Detach the torque arm from the brake back plate after removing the nut secured by a split pin. Unscrew the brake rod adjuster nut fully and depress the brake pedal so that the rod leaves the trunnion in the brake operating arm. Refit the nut to secure the rod spring.

4   Remove the wheel spindle nut after displacing the split pin. Withdraw the wheel spindle from the left-hand side and catch the right-hand spacer as it falls free. The sprocket, still meshed with the chain, can be pulled out, away from the hub to free the wheel. The cush drive hub will come away with the sprocket, leaving the cush drive rubber inserts in position. Tilt the wheel slightly and remove it from between the fork arms.

5   Refit the wheel by reversing the dismantling procedure. Ensure that the torque arm is secure and that the securing split pins are fitted. Likewise do not omit the wheel spindle nut securing pin. Before tightening the spindle nut, the final drive chain should be adjusted so that there is 20 – 30 mm (0.8 – 1.2 inch) up and down play measured in the centre of the chain lower run. Refer to the index marks on the fork ends when tightening the adjuster bolts, to ensure that wheel alignment is maintained.

11.1 Plastic dust cover is a tight push fit

11.2 Oil seals may be driven out with the bearing

11.4 Do not omit bearing spacer

12.3a Detach brake rod by removing adjuster nut and ...

12.3b ... disconnect torque arm

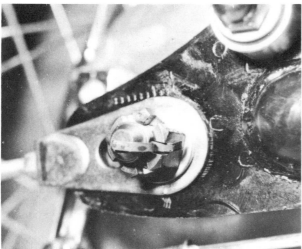

12.4a After removing split pin and nut withdraw the wheel spindle

12.4b Remove wheel from between the fork

12.5a Do not omit spacer on right or ...

12.5b ... left of wheel during reinstallation

13 Rear wheel drum brake: examination and renovation

1   After removal of the rear wheel, the brake plate complete with brake shoes can be removed from the wheel hub.
2   Examine the brake linings for oil, dirt or grease. Surface dirt can be removed with a stiff brush but oil soaked linings should be renewed. High spots can be carefully eased down with emery cloth.
3   Examine the condition of the brake linings and if they have worn thin they should be renewed. The brake linings are bonded to the brake shoes and thus separate linings are not available.
4   To remove the shoes pull them away from the cam and the brake plate in a V formation so that they can be removed together complete with the return springs. When they are well clear of the brake plate the springs can be removed. Check the springs for any signs of wear or stretching and renew if necessary. Check the surface of the brake drum for wear or scoring.
5   Whilst the brake plate is off, the brake cam spindle should be lubricated sparingly with grease. Mark the relative position of the brake operating arm and the splined end of the camshaft. Remove the pinch bolt and pull off the arm. The camshaft may be pushed out towards the inside of the back plate. Note the 'O' ring on the camshaft, which prevents the escape of grease. When refitting the camshaft and arm, realign the marks to restore the original position.
6   The brake drum should be checked for scoring. This happens if the brake shoe linings have been allowed to get too thin. The drums should be quite smooth. Remove all traces of lining dust and wipe with a clean rag soaked in petrol to remove all traces of grease and oil.
7   To reassemble the brake shoe on the brake plate, fit the return springs and pull the shoes apart, holding them in a V formation. If they are now located with the cam they can be pushed back into position. Do not use excessive force or there is a risk of distorting the shoes or over-stretching the springs.

14 Adjusting the rear brake

1   Adjustment of the rear brake is correct when there is 20 – 30 mm ($\frac{3}{4}$" – 1" approx) up and down movement measured at the rear brake pedal foot piece, between the fully off and on position.
2   If, when the brake is fully applied, the angle between the brake arm and the operating rod is more than 90°, the brake arm should be pulled off the camshaft, after loosening the pinch bolt. Reset the brake arm so that the right angle is produced.
3   Note that it may be necessary to adjust the height-setting of the stop lamp switch after adjustment of the brake pedal position.

15 Rear wheel bearings: removal and replacement

1   The rear wheel assembly has three journal ball bearings. One bearing lies each side of the wheel hub and the third bearing is fitted in the cush drive assembly to which is attached the sprocket.
2   The cush drive sprocket unit can be removed from engagement with the final drive chain after the rear wheel spindle has been withdrawn and the wheel lifted over to the right-hand side of the swinging arm fork.
3   Drift the wheel bearings from position using the same method as described for the front wheel. Before the cush drive bearing is tapped out, the hollow spindle should be removed. It is not necessary to remove the sprocket.
    The cush drive hub bearing oil seal may be drifted out at the same time as the bearing.

16 Rear cush drive: examination and renovation

1   The cush drive assembly is contained in the left-hand side of the wheel hub. It takes the form of six triangular rubber pads incorporating slots, that fit within the vanes of the hub. A heavily ribbed plate bolted to the rear sprocket engages with the slots to form a shock absorber which permits the sprocket to move within certain limits. This absorbs any surge or roughness in the transmission. The rubbers should be renewed when movement of the sprocket indicates bad compaction of the rubbers or if they commence to break up.

17 Rear wheel sprocket: examination and replacement

1   The rear wheel sprocket is held to the cush drive hub by six bolts locked by three tab washers. To remove the sprocket, bend back the locking tabs and undo the bolts. The sprocket need only be renewed if the teeth are worn or chipped. It is always a good policy to change both sprockets at the same time, together with the chain, otherwise the worn component will cause rapid wear of the new component(s).

16.1a Cush drive hub is a push fit in the rubbers

16.1b Do not omit shouldered spacer on reassembly

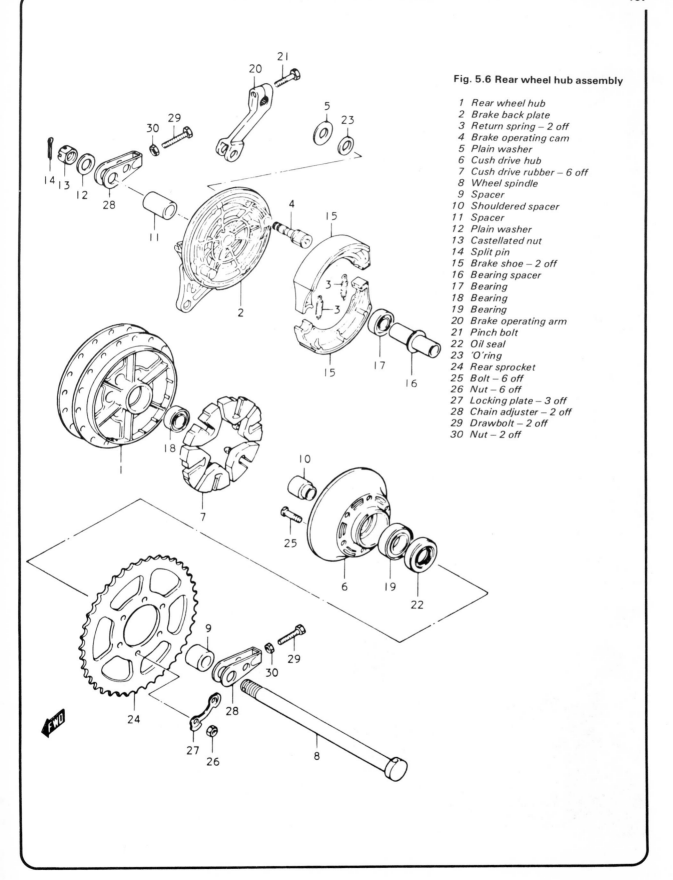

Fig. 5.6 Rear wheel hub assembly

1 Rear wheel hub
2 Brake back plate
3 Return spring – 2 off
4 Brake operating cam
5 Plain washer
6 Cush drive hub
7 Cush drive rubber – 6 off
8 Wheel spindle
9 Spacer
10 Shouldered spacer
11 Spacer
12 Plain washer
13 Castellated nut
14 Split pin
15 Brake shoe – 2 off
16 Bearing spacer
17 Bearing
18 Bearing
19 Bearing
20 Brake operating arm
21 Pinch bolt
22 Oil seal
23 'O'ring
24 Rear sprocket
25 Bolt – 6 off
26 Nut – 6 off
27 Locking plate – 3 off
28 Chain adjuster – 2 off
29 Drawbolt – 2 off
30 Nut – 2 off

18 Final drive chain: examination and lubrication

1   As the final drive chain is fully exposed on all models it requires lubrication and adjustment at regular intervals. To adjust the chain, take out the split pin from the rear wheel spindle and slacken the spindle nut. Slacken also the nuts securing the brake torque arm. Undo the locknut on the chain adjusters and turn the adjuster bolts inwards to tighten the chain. Marks on the adjusters must be in line with identical marks on the frame fork to align the rear wheel correctly. A final check can be made by laying a straight wooden plank alongside the wheels, each side in turn. Chain tension is correct if there is 15 – 20 mm (0.6 – 0.8 in) of slack in the middle of the chain run between the two sprockets.

A chain that is run exceptionally slack may strike the gear indicator switch which is retained on the gearbox wall. If the switch body breaks, lubricant loss from the gearbox may endanger the continued good health of the gearbox components. Do not run the chain overtight to compensate for uneven wear. A tight chain will place excessive stresses on the gearbox and rear wheel bearings leading to their early failure. It will also absorb a surprising amount of power.

2   After a period of running, the chain will require lubrication. Lack of oil will accelerate the rate of wear of both chain and sprockets and will lead to harsh transmission. The application of engine oil will act as a temporary expedient, but it is preferable to use one of the proprietary graphited greases contained within an aerosol can. This type of lubricant is thrown off the chain less easily than engine oil. Ideally the chain should be removed at regular intervals, and immersed in a molten lubricant such as Linklyfe or Chainguard after it has been cleaned in a paraffin bath. These latter lubricants achieve better penetration of the chain links and rollers and are less likely to be thrown off when the chain is in motion. If, however, the chain is of the original endless type, without a spring master link, the swinging arm must be removed to allow the chain to be detached.

3   As mentioned above, if the chain is of the original endless type, it is necessary to remove the complete swinging arm assembly in order to detach the chain for renewal. Refer to Chapter 4, Section 10.

4   To check if the chain is due for renewal, lay it length wise in a straight line and compress it endwise until all play is taken up. Anchor one end, then pull in the opposite direction to take up the play which has developed. If the chain extends by more than $\frac{1}{4}$ inch per foot it should be renewed. Note that this check should ALWAYS be made after the chain has been washed out, but before any lubricant is applied, otherwise the lubricant may take up some of the play.

18.1 Index marks on fork ends aid wheel alignment

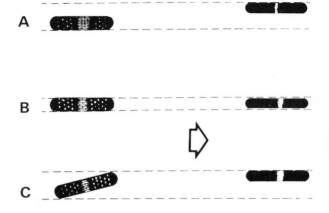

Fig. 5.7 Method of checking wheel alignment

A – Incorrect   *B – Correct*   *C – Incorrect*

19 Tyres: removal and replacement

1   At some time or other the need will arise to remove and replace the tyres, either as a result of a puncture or because replacements are necessary to offset wear. To the inexperienced, tyre changing represents a formidable task, yet if a few simple rules are observed and the technique learned, the whole operation is surprisingly simple.

2   To remove the tyre from either wheel, first detach the wheel from the machine. Deflate the tyre by removing the valve insert and when it is fully deflated, push the bead from the tyre away from the wheel rim on both sides so that the bead enters the centre well of the rim. Remove the locking cap and push the tyre valve into the tyre itself.

3   Insert a tyre lever close to the valve and lever the edge of the tyre over the outside of the wheel rim. Very little force should be necessary; if resistance is encountered it is probably due to the fact that the tyre beads have not entered the well of the wheel rim all the way round the tyre.

4   Once the tyre has been edged over the wheel rim, it is easy to work around the wheel rim so that the tyre is completely free on one side. At this stage, the inner tube can be removed.

5   Working from the other side of the wheel, ease the other edge of the tyre over the outside of the wheel rim that is furthest away. Continue to work around the rim until the tyre is free completely from the rim.

6   If a puncture has necessitated the removal of the tyre, reinflate the inner tube and immerse it in a bowl of water to trace the source of the leak. Mark its position and deflate the tube. Dry the tube and clean the area around the puncture with a petrol soaked rag. When the surface has dried, apply rubber solution and allow this to dry before removing the backing from the patch and applying the patch to the surface.

7   It is best to use a patch of self-vulcanising type, which will form a very permanent repair. Note that it may be necessary to remove a protective covering from the top surface of the patch, after it has sealed into position. Inner tubes made from synthetic rubber may require a special type of patch and adhesive, if a satisfactory bond is to be achieved.

8   Before refitting the tyre, check the inside to make sure that the object which caused the puncture is not trapped. Check the outside of the tyre, particularly the tread area, to make sure nothing is trapped that may cause a further puncture.

9   If the inner tube has been patched on a number of past occasions, or if there is a tear or large hole, it is preferable to

Tyre removal: Deflate inner tube and insert lever in close proximity to tyre valve

Use two levers to work bead over the edge of rim

When first bead is clear, remove tyre as shown

Tyre fitting: Inflate inner tube and insert in tyre

Lay tyre on rim and feed valve through hole in rim

Work first bead over rim, using lever in final section

Use similar technique for second bead, finish at tyre valve position

Push valve and tube up into tyre when fitting final section, to avoid trapping

discard it and fit a new one. Sudden deflation may cause an accident, particularly if it occurs with the front wheel.

10 To replace the tyre, inflate the inner tube sufficiently for it to assume a circular shape but only just. Then push it into the tyre so that it is enclosed completely. Lay the tyre on the wheel at an angle and insert the valve through the rim tape and the hole in the wheel rim. Attach the locking cap on the first few threads, sufficient to hold the valve captive in its correct location.

11 Starting at the point furthest from the valve, push the tyre bead over the edge of the wheel rim until it is located in the central well. Continue to work around the tyre in this fashion until the whole of one side of the tyre is on the rim. It may be necessary to use a tyre lever during the final stages.

12 Make sure that there is no pull on the tyre valve and again commencing with the area furthest from the valve, ease the other bead of the tyre over the edge of the rim. Finish with the area close to the valve, pushing the valve up into the tyre until the locking cap touches the rim. This will ensure the inner tube is not trapped when the last section of the bead is edged over the rim with a tyre lever.

13 Check that the inner tube is not trapped at any point. Reinflate the inner tube, and check that the tyre is seating correctly around the wheel rim. There should be a thin rib moulded around the wall of the tyre on both sides, which should be equidistant from the wheel rim at all points. If the tyre is unevenly located on the rim, try bouncing the wheel when the tyre is at the recommended pressure. It is probable that one of the beads has not pulled clear of the centre well.

14 Always run the tyres at the recommended pressures and never under or over-inflate. The correct pressures for solo use are given in the Specifications Section of this Chapter.

15 Tyre replacement is aided by dusting the side walls, particularly in the vicinity of the beads, with a liberal coating of french chalk. Washing-up liquid can also be used to good effect, but this has the disadvantage of causing the inner surfaces of the wheel rim to rust.

16 Never replace the inner tube and tyre without the rim tape in position. If this precaution is overlooked there is good chance of the ends of the spoke nipples chafing the inner tube and causing a crop of punctures.

17 Never fit a tyre that has a damaged tread or side walls. Apart from the legal aspects, there is a very great risk of a blow-out, which can have serious consequences on any two-wheel vehicle.

18 Tyre valves rarely give trouble, but it is always advisable to check whether the valve itself is leaking before removing the tyre. Do not forget to fit the dust cap, which forms an effective second seal.

20 Tyre valve dust caps

1 Tyre valve dust caps are often left off when a tyre has been replaced, despite the fact that they serve an important two-fold function. Firstly they prevent dirt or other foreign matter from entering the valve and causing the valve to stick open when the tyre pump is next applied. Secondly, they form an effective second seal so that in the event of the tyre valve sticking, air will not be lost.

2 Isolated cases of sudden deflation at high speeds have been traced to the omission of the dust cap. Centrifugal force has tended to lift the tyre valve off its seating and because the dust cap is missing, there has been no second seal. Racing inner tubes contain provision for this happening because the valve inserts are fitted with stronger springs, but standard inner tubes do not, hence the need for the dust cap.

3 Note that when a dust cap is fitted for the first time, the wheel may have to be rebalanced.

21 Front wheel: balancing

1 It is customary on all high performance machines to balance the front wheel complete with tyre and tube. The out of balance forces which exist are eliminated and the handling of the machine is improved in consequence. A wheel which is badly out of balance produces through the steering a most unpleasant hammering effect at high speeds.

2 Some tyres have a balance mark on the sidewall, usually in the form of a coloured dot. This mark must be in line with the tyre valve, when the tyre is fitted to the inner tube. Even then, the wheel may require the addition of balance weights, to offset the weight of the tyre valve itself.

3 If the front wheel is raised clear of the ground and is spun, it will come to rest with the tyre valve or the heaviest part downward and will always settle in the same position. Balance weights must be added to a point diametrically opposite this heavy spot until the wheel will come to rest in ANY position after it is spun.

4 Balance weights which clip around the wheel spokes are normally available in 20 or 30 gram sizes. If they are not available, wire solder, wrapped around the spokes close to the spoke nipples, forms a good substitute.

5 There is no necessity to balance the rear wheel under normal road conditions, although it is advisable to replace the rear wheel tyre so that any balance mark is in line with the tyre valve.

22 Fault diagnosis: wheels, brakes and tyres

Symptom	Cause	Remedy
Handlebars oscillate at low speed	Buckle or flat in wheel rim, most probably front wheel	Check rim alignment by spinning the wheel.
	Tyre not straight on rim	Correct by retensioning spokes or having wheel rebuilt on new rim. Check tyre alignment.
Machine lacks power and accelerates poorly	Brakes binding	Hot brake drum provides best evidence (drum brakes only).
	Wrongly adjusted caliper	Readjust caliper.
Brakes grab when applied gently	Ends of brake shoes not chamfered (drum brakes)	Chamfer with a file.
	Elliptical brake drum (drum brakes)	Lightly skim in a lathe by a specialist.
	Faulty caliper, on disc brake	Replace with a new caliper.
	Warped disc	Replace disc if beyond skimming limit.
Brake squeal	Glazed pads	Lightly sand the pads, and use the brake gently for a hundred miles or so until they have a chance to bed in properly.
	Extremely dirty and dusty front brake caliper and disc assembly	Clean with water; do not use high pressure spray equipment.
Excessive lever travel on front brake	Air in system, or leak in master cylinder or caliper; worn disc pads	Bleed the brake. Renew the cylinder seals. Renew the pads.
	Slack in cable (drum brakes only)	Adjust.

Chapter 6 Electrical system

Contents

Specifications

Battery
Make	Yuasa
Type	YB10L – A2
Voltage	12V
Capacity	10 ah
Earth	Negative

Alternator
Make	Nippon Denso or Kokusan
Type	12 coil stator, permanent magnet rotor
Output	14V, 14 amps at 8000 rpm
No load voltage	16·5 volts
Regulated voltage	14 – 15·5 volts

Voltage regulator
Type	SCR (silicon controlled solid state)

Rectifier
Type	Full-wave silicon

Starter motor
	Nippon Denso	or	Mitsuba
Make	Nippon Denso	or	Mitsuba
Voltage	11 volts		11 volts
Current (no load)	45 amps		50 amps
Brush length	14 mm (0·55 in)		12 – 13 mm (0·47 – 0·51 in)
Wear limit	9 mm (0·35 in)		6 mm (0·24 in)
Commutator undercut	0·6 mm (0·02 in)		0·6 mm (0·02 in)
Minimum undercut	0·2 mm (0·008 in)		0·2 mm (0·008 in)

Bulbs
Headlamps	45/45W	(40/30W USA)
Instrument lamp	3·4W	
Flasher pilot lamp	3·4W	
High-beam lamp	3·4W	
Neutral indicator lamp	3·4W	
Flashing indicator	23W x 4	
Tail/stop lamp	8/23W	(3/32 cp)

1 General description

The Suzuki GS 400 models are fitted with a 12 volt electrical system, powered by an alternator mounted on the extreme left-hand end of the crankshaft. The alternator, which produces alternating current, is of the three-stage type, having a permanent magnet rotor and a twelve-coil stator. During daylight running, when no lights are being used, only two of the three output stages are utilised. The third stage remains out of circuit until the lighting switch is operated, when additional current is required to meet the demands of the lighting circuit.

The ac current produced by the alternator is converted into dc current by a full-wave silicon rectifier and is controlled to meet the voltage demands of the system by a solid state regulator (SCR).

2 Testing the electrical system: general

1   Checking the electrical output and the performance of the various components within the charging system requires the use of test equipment of the multi-meter type. When carrying out checks, care must be taken to follow the procedures laid down and so prevent inadvertent incorrect connections or short circuits. Irreparable damage to individual components may result if reversal of current or shorting occurs. It is advised that unless some previous experience has been gained in auto-electrical testing, the machine be returned to a Suzuki Service Agent or auto-electrician, who will be qualified to carry out the work and have the necessary test equipment.
2   If the performance of the charging system is suspect, the system as a whole should be checked first, followed by testing of the individual components to isolate the fault. The three main components are the alternator, the rectifier, and the regulator. Before commencing the tests, ensure that the battery is fully charged, as described in Section 7.

3 Charging system: checking the output

1st test

1   The first test is performed in a no-load state, with the regulator disconnected, and will verify whether the alternator and rectifier are functioning. Raise the dualseat so that access may be made to the wiring harness.
2   Disconnect the yellow wire running from the regulator. Disconnect the white/green wire running from the alternator and the white/red wire from the rectifier. Connect these two wires together to by-pass the lighting switch. Turn the lighting switch off. Connect a 0-20v dc voltmeter across the battery terminals. Start the engine and increase the speed to 5000 rpm. At this speed the indicated voltage should be 16.5 volts or over. If the voltage is below 16.5 volts the alternator or the rectifier is faulty. To eliminate the faulty component refer to Section 4 or 5 of this Chapter.

2nd test

3   If the first test proved that both the alternator and rectifier are functioning correctly, the second test should be carried out to determine the performance of the regulator. Reconnect the wires so that they are restored to their original positions. Turn the lighting switch off so that only two of the three output stages are in circuit. On models supplied to the USA, where the lighting switch is locked in the On position, remove the switch knob and turn the switch off.
4   Start the engine and again check the voltage at 5000 rpm. If the indicated voltage is within the range 14.0 – 15.5 volts the regulator is functioning correctly. A reading above or below this range indicates that the regulator is faulty. Before consigning the regulator to the scrap bin, check that all the wiring connections are clean and tight. Again check that the battery is fully

charged and repeat the test. A replacement regulator must be of the same make as the alternator.

4 Rectifier: location and testing

1   The rectifier is fitted behind the left-hand side cover to the rear of the regulator. If the rectifier is suspected of being faulty after carrying out test No 1 in the preceding Section, it may be tested in situ using a multi-meter set to the resistance function.
2   Disconnect the battery to isolate the electrical system and then disconnect all five wires which lead to the rectifier unit. Connect the negative ohmmeter lead to the regulator earth terminal (black/white) and then test the continuity between the earth and the following terminals: yellow, white/red, white/blue. Continuity should be indicated on each. Reverse the polarity of the ohmmeter and repeat the test. No continuity should be indicated. Carry out the same series of tests but with the output terminal (red) used as the common test terminal, in place of the earth terminal. The correct results should be the reverse of those given for the first part of the test. If one or more incorrect readings is found, the rectifier must be renewed.

5 Alternator: testing

1   If after carrying out test No 1 in Section 3 of this Chapter it was found that the alternator or rectifier was not functioning correctly, as indicated by the voltage reading, the alternator may be tested after removal of the stator from the machine, using a multi-meter set to the resistance function.
2   Disconnect the leads running from the alternator and check the continuity between the three wires, making the test in pairs. The correct resistance is 0.65 ohms $\pm$ 0.05%. If there is found to be no continuity between any two of the wires, or if the resistance is too low, a short-circuit or open-circuit is evident, and the stator must be renewed. Two makes of alternator are utilised, Denso and Kokusan. When renewing the stator, ensure that the replacement component is of the same manufacture as the rotor.
3   Check the resistance between each wire and the stator core. No continuity should be found.

6 Battery: examination and maintenance

1   Both models are fitted with a 12 volt battery of which the GS400B has a 10 ampere hour capacity and the GS400XB has a 7 ampere hour capacity.
2   The transparent plastic case of the battery permits the upper and lower levels of the electrolyte to be observed without disturbing the battery by removing the left-hand side cover. Maintenance is normally limited to keeping the electrolyte level between the prescribed upper and lower limits and making sure that the vent tube is not blocked. The lead plates and their separators are also visible through the transparent case, a further guide to the general condition of the battery.
3   Unless acid is spilt, as may occur if the machine falls over, the electrolyte should always be topped up with distilled water to restore the correct level. If acid is spilt onto any part of the machine, it should be neutralised with an alkali such as washing soda or baking powder and washed away with plenty of water, otherwise serious corrosion will occur. Top up- with sulphuric acid of the correct specific gravity (1.260 to 1.280) only when spillage has occurred. Check that the vent pipe is well clear of the frame or any of the other cycle parts.
4   It is seldom practicable to repair a cracked battery case because the acid present in the joint will prevent the formation of an effective seal. It is always best to renew a cracked battery, especially in view of the corrosion which will be caused if the acid continues to leak.
5   If the machine is not used for a period, it is advisable to remove the battery and give it a refresher charge every six

weeks or so from a battery charger. If the battery is permitted to discharge completely, the plates will sulphate and render the battery useless.

6   Occasionally, check the condition of the battery terminals to ensure that corrosion is not taking place and that the electrical connections are tight. If corrosion has occurred, it should be cleaned away by scraping with a knife and then using emery cloth to remove the final traces. Remake the electrical connections whilst the joint is still clean, then smear the assembly with petroleum jelly (NOT grease) to prevent recurrence of the corrosion. Badly corroded connections can have a high electrical resistance and may give the impression of a complete battery failure.

7   Battery: charging procedure

1   The normal charging rate for batteries of up to 14 amp. hour capacity is $1\frac{1}{2}$ amps. It is permissible to charge at a more rapid rate in an emergency but this shortens the life of the battery, and should be avoided. Always remove the vent caps when recharging a battery, otherwise the gas created within the battery when charging takes place will explode and burst the case with disastrous consequences.

8   Fuse: location and replacement

1   A fuse is incorporated in the electrical system. It is contained in a plastic holder located below the dualseat. The fuse is incorporated in the system to give protection from a sudden overload such as could happen with a short circuit. The fuse is rated at 15 amps.
2   If the fuse blows it should not be renewed until the cause of the short is found. This will involve checking the electrical circuit to correct the fault. If this rule is not observed, the fuse will almost certainly blow again.
3   When a fuse blows and no spare is available a get you home remedy is to wrap the fuse in silver paper before replacing it in the fuse holder. The silver paper will restore electrical continuity by bridging the broken wire within the fuse. Replace the doctored fuse at the earliest opportunity to restore full circuit protection. Make sure any short circuit is eliminated first.
4   Always carry two spare fuses of the correct rating.

5.2 Alternator coils may be checked using resistance meter

9   Starter motor: removal, examination and replacement – GS400B and C models only

1   An electric starter motor, operated from a small push-button on the right-hand side of the handlebars, provides an alternative and more convenient method of starting the engine, without having to use the kickstart. The starter motor is mounted within a compartment at the rear of the cylinder block, closed by an oblong, chromium plated cover. Current is supplied from the battery via a heavy duty solenoid switch and a cable capable of carrying the very high current demanded by the starter motor on the initial start-up.
2   The starter motor drives a free running clutch immediately behind the generator rotor. The clutch ensures the starter motor drive is disconnected from the crankshaft immediately the engine starts. It operates on the centrifugal principle; spring loaded rollers take up the drive until the centrifugal force of the rotating engine overcomes their resistance and the drive is automatically disconnected.
3   To remove the starter motor from the engine unit, first disconnect the positive lead from the battery, to isolate the electrical system. Remove the cover plate which encloses the

6.1 Remove side panel to gain access to battery

8.1 The fuse is contained in a white plastic pod

starter motor and detach the heavy duty cable from the terminal on the starter motor body. The starter motor is secured to the crankcase by two bolts which pass through the left-hand end of the motor casting. When these bolts are withdrawn, the motor can be prised out of position and lifted out of its compartment.

4   The parts of the starter motor most likely to require attention are the brushes. The end cover is retained by the two long screws which pass through the lugs cast on both end pieces. If the screws are withdrawn, the end cover can be lifted away and the brush gear exposed.

5   Lift up the spring clips which bear on the end of each brush and remove the brushes from their holders. The standard length and wear limit of the brushes depends on the make of starter motor employed, as follows:

	standard length	service limit
Mitsuba	12–13 mm	6 mm
	(0.47–0.51 in)	(0.24 in)
Denso	14 mm	9 mm
	(0.55 in)	(0.35 in)

6   Before the brushes are replaced, make sure the commutator on which they bear is clean. Clean with a strip of fine glass paper cloth pressed against the commutator whilst the latter is revolved by hand.

Emery paper should **NOT** be used because abrasive fragments may embed themselves in the soft metal of the commutator and cause excessive wear of the brushes. Finish off the commutator with metal polish to give a smooth surface and finally wipe the segments over with a methylated spirits soaked rag to ensure a grease free surface. Check that the mica insulators, which lie between the segments of the commutator, are undercut. The standard groove depth is 0.6 mm (0.02 in) but if the average groove depth is less than 0.2 mm (0.008 in)

the armature should be renewed or returned to a Suzuki Service Agent for re-cutting.

7   Replace the brushes in their holders and check that they slide quite freely. Make sure the brushes are replaced in their original positions because they will have worn to the profile of the commutator. Replace and tighten the end cover, then replace the starter motor and cable in the housing, tighten down and re-make the electrical connection to the solenoid switch. Check that the starter motor functions correctly before replacing the compartment cover and sealing gasket.

10 Starter motor free running clutch: construction and renovation – GS400B and C models only

1   Although a mechanical and not an electrical component, it is appropriate to include the free running clutch in this Chapter because it is an essential part of the electric starter system.

2   As mentioned in Chapter 1, the free running clutch is built into the alternator rotor assembly and will be found in the back of the rotor when the latter is removed from the left-hand end of the crankshaft. The only parts likely to require attention are the rollers and their springs, or the bearings in the centre of the driven sprocket. Access to the rollers is gained by removing the three countersunk crosshead screws which retain the clutch body to the rear of the alternator rotor. Signs of wear or damage will be obvious and will necessitate renewal of the worn or damaged parts.

3   The bearings in the centre of the driven sprocket behind the clutch will need renewal only after very extensive service.

4   To check whether the clutch is operating correctly, turn the driven sprocket anti-clockwise. This should force the spring loaded rollers against the crankshaft and cause it to tighten on the crankshaft as the drive is taken up.

5   If the starter clutch has been dismantled, make sure the three crosshead screws are staked over after reassembly, to prevent their working loose.

1   Armature
2   Brush holder unit
3   Brush set
4   Shim set
5   Bolt – 2 off
6   'O'ring – 2 off
7   Bolt – 2 off
8   'O'ring
9   Nut
10   Spring washer

*Fig. 6.1 Starter motor

* Motor shown is a Mitsuba component. Nippon Denso components are also used. These are similar in construction

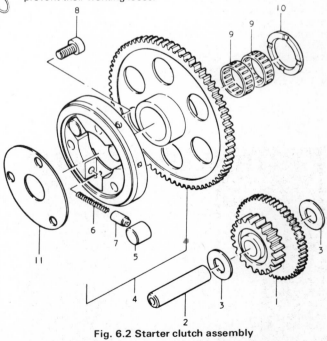

Fig. 6.2 Starter clutch assembly

1 Intermediate pinion	7 Plunger – 3 off
2 Spindle	8 Socket screw – 3 off
3 Thrust washer – 2 off	9 Needle roller bearing – 2 off
4 Starter clutch assembly	10 Bronze thrust washer
5 Roller – 3 off	11 Endplate
6 Spring – 3 off	

10.2 Check rollers for scoring and plungers for sticking

11 Starter solenoid switch: function and location – GS400B and C models only

1   The starter motor switch is designed to work on the electro-magnetic principle. When the starter motor button is depressed, current from the battery passes through windings in the switch solenoid and generates an electro-magnetic force which causes a set of contact points to close. Immediately the points close, the starter motor is energised and a very heavy current is drawn from the battery.

2   This arrangement is used for two reasons. Firstly, the starter motor current is drawn only when the button is depressed and is cut off again when pressure on the button is released. This ensures minimum drainage on the battery. Secondly, if the battery is in a low state of charge, there will not be sufficient current to cause the solenoid contacts to close. In consequence, it is not possible to place an excessive drain on the battery which, in some circumstances, can cause the plates to overheat and shed their coatings. If the starter will not operate, first suspect a discharged battery. This can be checked by trying the horn or switching on the lights. If this check shows the battery to be in good shape, suspect the starter switch which should come into action with a pronounced click. It is located under the dualseat, close to the battery, and can be identified by the heavy duty starter cable connected to it. It is not possible to effect a satisfactory repair if the switch malfunctions; it must be renewed.

12 Headlamp: replacing bulbs and adjusting beam height

1   In order to gain access to the headlamp bulbs it is necessary first to remove the rim, complete with the reflector and headlamp glass. The rim is retained by three crosshead screws equally spaced around the headlamp shell. Remove the screws completely and draw the rim from the headlamp shell.

2   UK models have a main headlamp bulb which is a push fit into the central bulb holder of the reflector. The bulb holder can be replaced in one position only to ensure the bulb is always correctly focussed. It is retained by a bayonet fitting. A bulb of the twin filament type is fitted which has a 45/45W rating. The pilot lamp bulb is bayonet fitting and fits within a bulb holder which has the same form of attachment to the headlamp reflector. This bulb has a 6W rating.

3   US models have a sealed beam headlamp unit, rated at 40/35W with no provision for a pilot lamp. If one filament blows, the complete unit must be renewed. To release the lamp

unit, remove the horizontal adjusting screw, the upper and lower retaining lock pins and screws from the collar which clamps the light unit to the headlamp rim. Make a note of the setting of the adjusting screw, otherwise it will be necessary to re-adjust the beam height after installing the new light unit by reversing the dismantling procedure.

4   Beam height on all models is effected by tilting the headlamp shell after the mounting bolts have been loosened slightly. On sealed beam units the horizontal alignment of the beam can be adjusted by altering the position of the screw which passes through the headlamp rim. The screw is fitted at the 9 o'clock position when viewed from the front of the machine. Turning the screw in a clockwise direction will move the beam direction over to the left-hand side.

5   UK lighting regulations stipulate that the lighting system must be arranged so that the light will not dazzle a person standing at a distance greater than 25 feet from the lamp, whose eye level is not less than 3 feet 6 inches above that plane. It is easy to approximate this setting by placing the machine 25 feet away from a wall, on a level road, and setting the beam height so that it is concentrated at the same height as the distance of the centre of the headlamp from the ground. The rider must be seated normally during this operation and also the pillion passenger, if one is carried regularly.

13 Stop and tail lamp: replacing bulbs

1   The tail lamp has a twin filament bulb of 8/23W (3/32 cp) to illuminate the rear number plate and to indicate when the rear brake is applied. On some models the stop lamp also operates in conjunction with the front brake; a stop lamp switch may be incorporated in the front brake lever to meet the statutory requirements of the country or state to which the machine is exported.

2   To gain access to the stop and tail lamp bulb, unscrew the four crosshead screws which retain the plastic lens cover in position. The bulb has a bayonet fitting and offset pins so that the stop lamp filament cannot be inadvertently connected with the tail lamp and vice versa.

14 Flashing indicator lamps: replacing bulbs

1   Flashing indicator lamps are fitted to the front and rear of the machine. They are mounted on short stalks through which the wires pass. Access to each bulb is gained by removing the two screws holding the plastic lens cover. The bulbs are of 23W rating and are retained by a bayonet fixing.

11.1 A = Starter solenoid, B= Rectifier, C = Regulator, D= Flasher unit

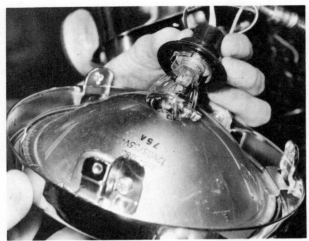

12.2a Bayonet fitting bulb is secured in twist fit bulb holder

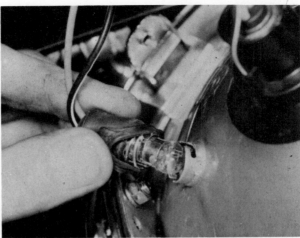

12.2b Pilot bulb holder has bayonet fitting as does bulb

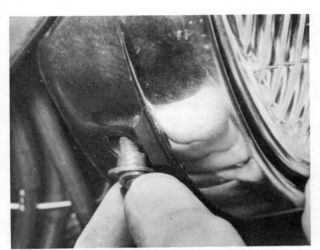

12.2c Note insert on reflector unit holding screw

13.1 Stop/tail lamp lens has four retaining screws

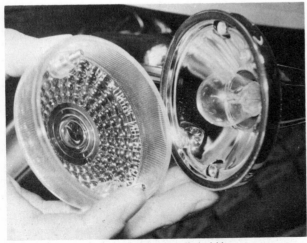

14.1 Each flashing indicator lamp lens is held by two screws

15 Instrument and warning bulbs: replacement

1   The bulbs fitted to the instrument heads and the warning light panel (late models) are of the small bayonet type, the holders being a push fit in the underside of the brackets. Replacement of bulbs in the warning panel first requires that the lower cover be removed. It is retained by the two sets of two nuts which secure the instruments to the mounting bracket.

16 Horn: adjustments

1   On some models the horn is adjustable by means of a small grub screw at the back of the body so that the volume can be varied if necessary. To adjust the volume, loosen the locknut, turn the screw about half a turn either way until the desired tone is required. After adjustment tighten the locknut.

2   The horn button is located on the left side of the handlebars, below the dip switch.

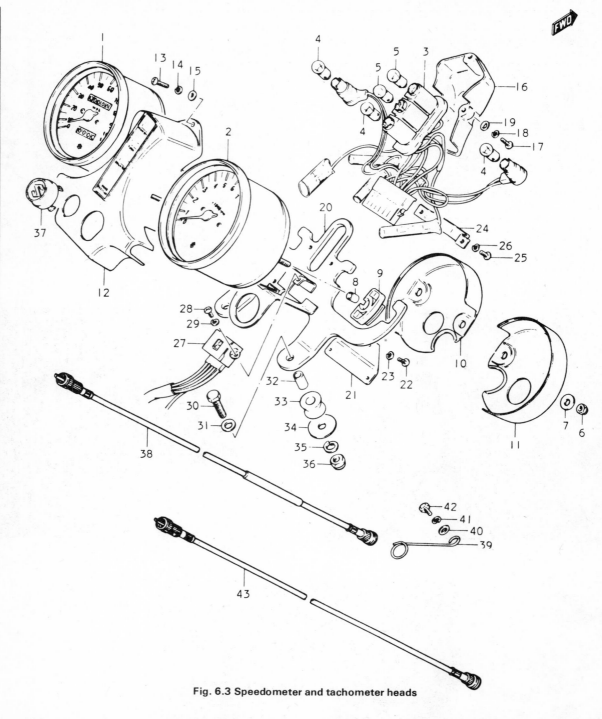

Fig. 6.3 Speedometer and tachometer heads

1 Speedometer head
2 Tachometer head
3 Bulb holder unit
4 Bulb – 3 off
5 Bulb – 2 off
6 Domed nut – 4 off
7 Washer – 4 off
8 Spacer – 4 off
9 Damper rubber – 4 off
10 Speedometer cover
11 Tachometer cover

12 Warning bulb cover
13 Screw
14 Spring washer
15 Plain washer
16 Bulb lower cover
17 Screw – 2 off
18 Spring washer – 2 off
19 Plain washer – 2 off
20 Instrument bracket
21 Retainer plate
22 Screw

23 Spring washer
24 Block connector bracket
25 Screw – 2 off
26 Spring washer – 2 off
27 Gear Position Digital Display Unit
28 Screw – 2 off
29 Spring washer – 2 off
30 Bolt – 3 off
31 Plain washer – 2 off
32 Spacer – 2 off

33 Grommet – 2 off
34 Plain washer – 2 off
35 Spring washer – 2 off
36 Domed nut – 2 off
37 Plug
38 Speedometer drive cable
39 Cable guide
40 Plain washer
41 Spring washer
42 Bolt
43 Tachometer drive cable

17 Handlebar switches, ignition and lighting switches: examination

1   The arrangement of the handlebar switches is the same on all models. The switches seldom give any trouble; they can be separated by removing the two screws that hold the two halves together. It is not advisable to take the switches apart as the parts are small and difficulties can occur during reassembly. If a switch fails, it is best to fit a new replacement.

2   The ignition switch is located in the centre of the instrument panel. It can be removed by undoing the locking ring or bezel on the body. The wires can be pulled out of the socket and the new switch plugged in. New keys are supplied with a new switch. A defective switch is not repairable.

18 Stop lamp switch: adjustment

1   The stop lamp switch is located in a bracket above the rear brake pedal and is operated by an extension spring linked to the rear brake pedal. The body of the switch is threaded to permit it to be adjusted.

2   If the stop lamp is late in operating, slacken the locknuts and raise the switch body. When the adjustment seems correct tighten locknuts and test. If the stop lamp is too early in operation, slacken the locknuts and lower the body in relation to the bracket.

3   As a guide, the light should come on when the rear brake pedal has been depressed about 2 cm ($\frac{3}{4}$ in).

19 Gear selection indicator: location and operation

1   A gear selection indicator is fitted to all models in addition to the neutral warning light. In this system, a switch on the change drum illuminates a single digit display unit fitted in a console between the speedometer and tachometer heads. The display unit is similar to that used on pocket calculators and indicates which of the gears has been selected. If a malfunction occurs, the unit in question must be renewed as both components are sealed. On all models, the neutral warning bulb can be replaced as with the other warning bulbs fitted to the instrument heads.

15.1 Remove lower cover to gain access to warning bulbs

16.1 Horn tone may be adjusted by small screw

18.2 Stop lamp switch may be adjusted by raising or lowering body

20 Fault diagnosis: electrical system

Symptom	Cause	Remedy
Complete electrical failure	Blown fuse	Check wiring and electrical components for short circuit before fitting new 15 amp fuse.
	Isolated battery	Check battery connections, also whether connections show signs of corrosion.
Dim lights, horn and starter inoperative	Discharged battery	Remove battery and charge with battery charger. Check generator output and voltage regulator performance.
Constantly blowing bulbs	Vibration or poor earth connection	Check security of bulb holders. Check earth connections.
Parking lights dim rapidly	Battery will not hold charge	Renew battery at earliest opportunity.
Flashing indicators do not operate	Blown bulb	Renew bulb.
	Damaged flasher unit	Renew flasher unit.

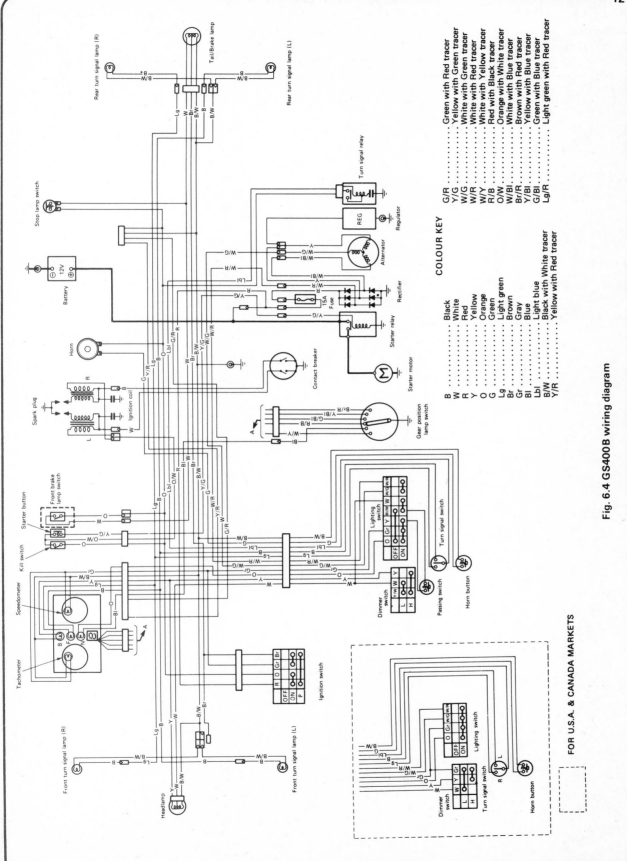

Fig. 6.4 GS400B wiring diagram

FOR U.S.A. & CANADA MARKETS

COLOUR KEY

B	Black	
W	White	
R	Red	
Y	Yellow	
O	Orange	
G	Green	
Lg	Light green	
Br	Brown	
Gr	Gray	
Bl	Blue	
Lbl	Light blue	
B/W	Black with White tracer	
Y/R	Yellow with Red tracer	

G/R	Green with Red tracer	
Y/G	Yellow with Green tracer	
W/G	White with Green tracer	
W/R	White with Red tracer	
W/Y	White with Yellow tracer	
R/B	Red with Black tracer	
O/W	Orange with White tracer	
W/Bl	White with Blue tracer	
Br/R	Brown with Red tracer	
Y/Bl	Yellow with Blue tracer	
G/Bl	Green with Blue tracer	
Lg/R	Light green with Red tracer	

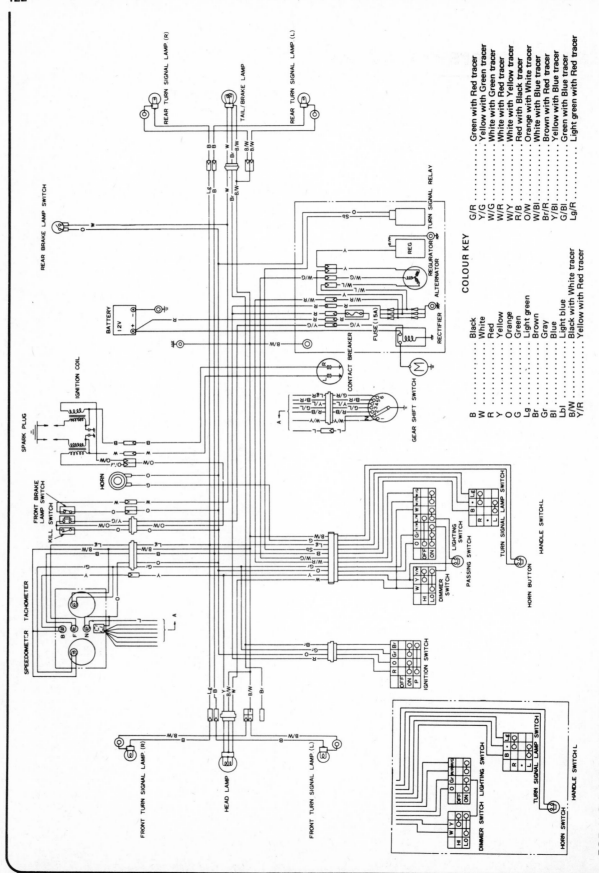

Fig. 6.5 Suzuki GS400C Wiring diagram

FOR U.S.A & CANADA MARKETS

Metric conversion tables

Inches	Decimals	Millimetres	Millimetres to Inches		Inches to Millimetres	
			mm	Inches	Inches	mm
1/64	0.015625	0.3969	0.01	0.00039	0.001	0.0254
1/32	0.03125	0.7937	0.02	0.00079	0.002	0.0508
3/64	0.046875	1.1906	0.03	0.00118	0.003	0.0762
1/16	0.0625	1.5875	0.04	0.00157	0.004	0.1016
5/64	0.078125	1.9844	0.05	0.00197	0.005	0.1270
3/32	0.09375	2.3812	0.06	0.00236	0.006	0.1524
7/64	0.109375	2.7781	0.07	0.00276	0.007	0.1778
1/8	0.125	3.1750	0.08	0.00315	0.008	0.2032
9/64	0.140625	3.5719	0.09	0.00354	0.009	0.2286
5/32	0.15625	3.9687	0.1	0.00394	0.01	0.254
11/64	0.171875	4.3656	0.2	0.00787	0.02	0.508
3/16	0.1875	4.7625	0.3	0.01181	0.03	0.762
13/64	0.203125	5.1594	0.4	0.01575	0.04	1.016
7/32	0.21875	5.5562	0.5	0.01969	0.05	1.270
15/64	0.234375	5.9531	0.6	0.02362	0.06	1.524
1/4	0.25	6.3500	0.7	0.02756	0.07	1.778
17/64	0.265625	6.7469	0.8	0.03150	0.08	2.032
9/32	0.28125	7.1437	0.9	0.03543	0.09	2.286
19/64	0.296875	7.5406	1	0.03937	0.1	2.54
5/16	0.3125	7.9375	2	0.07874	0.2	5.08
21/64	0.328125	8.3344	3	0.11811	0.3	7.62
11/32	0.34375	8.7312	4	0.15748	0.4	10.16
23/64	0.359375	9.1281	5	0.19685	0.5	12.70
3/8	0.375	9.5250	6	0.23622	0.6	15.24
25/64	0.390625	9.9219	7	0.27559	0.7	17.78
13/32	0.40625	10.3187	8	0.31496	0.8	20.32
27/64	0.421875	10.7156	9	0.35433	0.9	22.86
7/16	0.4375	11.1125	10	0.39370	1	25.4
29/64	0.453125	11.5094	11	0.43307	2	50.8
15/32	0.46875	11.9062	12	0.47244	3	76.2
31/64	0.48375	12.3031	13	0.51181	4	101.6
1/2	0.5	12.7000	14	0.55118	5	127.0
33/64	0.515625	13.0969	15	0.59055	6	152.4
17/32	0.53125	13.4937	16	0.62992	7	177.8
35/64	0.546875	13.8906	17	0.66929	8	203.2
9/16	0.5625	14.2875	18	0.70866	9	228.6
37/64	0.578125	14.6844	19	0.74803	10	254.0
19/32	0.59375	15.0812	20	0.78740	11	279.4
39/64	0.609375	15.4781	21	0.82677	12	304.8
5/8	0.625	15.8750	22	0.86614	13	330.2
41/64	0.640625	16.2719	23	0.90551	14	355.6
21/32	0.65625	16.6687	24	0.94488	15	381.0
43/64	0.671875	17.0656	25	0.98425	16	406.4
11/16	0.6875	17.4625	26	1.02362	17	431.8
45/64	0.703125	17.8594	27	1.06299	18	457.2
23/32	0.71875	18.2562	28	1.10236	19	482.6
47/64	0.734375	18.6531	29	1.14173	20	508.0
3/4	0.75	19.0500	30	1.18110	21	533.4
49/64	0.765625	19.4469	31	1.22047	22	558.8
25/32	0.78125	19.8437	32	1.25984	23	584.2
51/64	0.796875	20.2406	33	1.29921	24	609.6
13/16	0.8125	20.6375	34	1.33858	25	635.0
53/64	0.828125	21.0344	35	1.37795	26	660.4
27/32	0.84375	21.4312	36	1.41732	27	685.8
55/64	0.859375	21.8281	37	1.4567	28	711.2
7/8	0.875	22.2250	38	1.4961	29	736.6
57/64	0.890625	22.6219	39	1.5354	30	762.0
29/32	0.90625	23.0187	40	1.5748	31	787.4
59/64	0.921875	23.4156	41	1.6142	32	812.8
15/16	0.9375	23.8125	42	1.6535	33	838.2
61/64	0.953125	24.2094	43	1.6929	34	863.6
31/32	0.96875	24.6062	44	1.7323	35	889.0
63/64	0.984375	25.0031	45	1.7717	36	914.4

Metric Conversion Tables

1   Imperial gallon = 8 Imp pints = 1.16 US gallons = 277.42 cu in = 4.5459 litres

1   US gallon = 4 US quarts = 0.862 Imp gallon = 231 cu in = 3.785 litres

1   Litre = 0.2199 Imp gallon = 0.2642 US gallon = 61.0253 cu in = 1000 cc

Miles to Kilometres		Kilometres to Miles	
1	1.61	1	0.62
2	3.22	2	1.24
3	4.83	3	1.86
4	6.44	4	2.49
5	8.05	5	3.11
6	9.66	6	3.73
7	11.27	7	4.35
8	12.88	8	4.97
9	14.48	9	5.59
10	16.09	10	6.21
20	32.19	20	12.43
30	48.28	30	18.64
40	64.37	40	24.85
50	80.47	50	31.07
60	96.56	60	37.28
70	112.65	70	43.50
80	128.75	80	49.71
90	144.84	90	55.92
100	160.93	100	62.14

lb f ft to Kg f m		Kg f m to lb f ft		lb f/in^2 : Kg f/cm^2		Kg f/cm^2 : lb f/in^2	
1	0.138	1	7.233	1	0.07	1	14.22
2	0.276	2	14.466	2	0.14	2	28.50
3	0.414	3	21.699	3	0.21	3	42.67
4	0.553	4	28.932	4	0.28	4	56.89
5	0.691	5	36.165	5	0.35	5	71.12
6	0.829	6	43.398	6	0.42	6	85.34
7	0.967	7	50.631	7	0.49	7	99.56
8	1.106	8	57.864	8	0.56	8	113.79
9	1.244	9	65.097	9	0.63	9	128.00
10	1.382	10	72.330	10	0.70	10	142.23
20	2.765	20	144.660	20	1.41	20	284.47
30	4.147	30	216.990	30	2.11	30	426.70

Index

Printed by
Haynes Publishing Group
Sparkford Yeovil Somerset
England